HE SPOKE TO US

GEORGE WILLIAM RUTLER

He Spoke to Us

Discerning God
in People and Events

FOREWORD BY EDWARD SHORT

IGNATIUS PRESS   SAN FRANCISCO

Cover art:

*Landscape with Christ and His Disciples
on the Road to Emmaus*
Jan Wildens (1586–1653)
The Hermitage, St. Petersburg, Russia

Cover design by Davin Carlson

© 2016 by Ignatius Press, San Francisco
All rights reserved
ISBN 978-1-58617-983-0
Library of Congress Control Number 2014949943
Printed in the United States of America ∞

CONTENTS

Father George Rutler *In Excelsio*

Recently, in search of light summer reading, I decided to dip into Tobias Smollet's *The Expedition of Humphry Clinker* (1771)—a book I had not opened since my antediluvian twenties—and I came upon a passage describing divines on vacation that reconfirmed all of my old admiration for the unsparing Georgian satirist.

> The musick and entertainments of Bath are over for this season; and all our gay birds of passage have taken their flight to Bristolwell, Tunbridge, Brighthelmstone, Scarborough, Harrowgate, &c. Not a soul is seen in this place, but a few broken-winded parsons, waddling like so many crows along the North Parade. There is always a great shew of the clergy at Bath: none of your thin, puny, yellow, hectic figures, exhausted with abstinence and hardy study, labouring under the *morbi eruditorum*, but great overgrown dignitaries and rectors, with rubicund noses and gouty ancles, or broad bloated faces, dragging along great swag bellies; the emblems of sloth and indigestion.

By contrast, I thought of the subject of this foreword, the Reverend George Rutler, a spry, athletic, ebullient man, who, far from laboring under any *morbi eruditorum*, is positively suffused with the joy of learning, especially when it helps him to illuminate the love of God, what Blessed John Henry Newman called "the one thing needful".

Many of my readers will know Father Rutler as the New York pastor who brought pastoral vitality and administrative aplomb, first, to the Church of Our Saviour on Park Avenue and, then, to the Church of Saint Michael on West Thirty-Fourth Street. Others will know him as

7

the witty proponent of faith and reason on EWTN or the author of many entertaining and instructive books, including his most recent, the highly acclaimed *Powers and Principalities*, a brilliantly original study of the Second World War, which exhibits an understanding of the moral uses of history that far too many professional historians either travesty or neglect. The Father Rutler of whom I should like to speak here is the writer of essays, a form of writing perfectly suited to his supple, far-ranging, discriminating wit.

In sharing with his readers his uncommonly insightful views of history, literature, society, and the faith, to name just a few of the subjects essayed in this collection, Father Rutler shows why he continues to exert such a formative influence not only over the faithful and the unfaithful but on those most difficult customers of all, the formerly faithful. It is to the last of these that the piece that opens the collection is addressed, a rather sobering piece, entitled, "The Transfiguration of the Church".

> Perfectionists are easily scandalized by what is not good. Saints are only scandalized by what is not glorious. We may say in cliché, "Nobody's perfect", but the fact is, saints are perfect, and they are precisely so because they do not try to be good, better, and best. On the contrary, the more they are transfigured by the Light, the more they seem to themselves bad, worse, and worst.

How frequently we hear lapsed Catholics giving out that they have lost faith in God's Church because they have lost faith in his less than perfect servants. For the benefit of these misguided precisians, Father Rutler offers useful home truths.

> In his last Angelus address, Benedict XVI said that he is now going up the mountain as did Peter, James, and John, and there he will pray. He knows that at the foot of the mountain are all kinds of noise and foaming, and these are the growls of the Prince of Darkness paying the Church a tribute he pays no other reality: his hatred. While he mocks men and scorns their pretensions, he reserves his bitterness for the Church, which is the only thing he fears in this world.

Besides hitting its target with pinpoint accuracy, this passage is characteristic of the essays as a whole in having the grace of good conversation. And this calls to mind another of Father Rutler's virtues: he is an enviably deft polemicist, who never allows the follies or the provocations of his subjects to disconcert his serene gunnery. For the sort of rhetorical poise that I have in mind, readers should see the essay here entitled "The Moral Exploitation of Penguins", which confounds those who defend what they imagine the moral acceptability of unnatural unions with marvelous suavity. No one in our time has come to the defense of truth with so much good sense or good humor as Father Rutler.

This readiness to champion truth necessarily involves the author in animadversions on our public men, many of whom treat truth as an infinitely malleable thing. In "The Shore of Tripoli", Father Rutler points out how President Obama wildly misrepresents Thomas Jefferson's view of Muslims. He also points out how ignorance of early American history is not the president's only blind spot.

Another essay here, "Governor Pliny and Governor Cuomo", in response to Andrew Cuomo telling pro-life and pro-marriage New Yorkers that they are unwelcome in the Empire State because they do not share the governor's fondness for abortion and homosexual marriage, is an equally good case in point. When the politicians of New York distort the truth, which they do with an almost compulsive frequency, the Catholic clergy of New York are not always quick to refute them. That Father Rutler takes the time to call these erring oracles to account shows what true Christian charity animates the man. Certainly, he has done the governor an immense service by pointing out to him how his readiness to insult and indeed persecute his opponents vitiates his government, not to mention what ought to be his obedience to the faith of his fathers. Then, again, that Father Rutler calls the governor to account with witty reference to Pliny and Trajan puts the misconduct of the present State of New York in a wider, historical context. And since history for Father Rutler is never a matter of barren antiquarianism but a living guide to sound moral judgment and sound moral action, his invocations of history are always of great practical import. Plutarch would approve.

Indeed, by giving Governor Cuomo and his administration the benefit of his own sound moral judgment, Father Rutler exemplifies something Cardinal Newman once wrote about the Church in her relation to the State, with which I am sure he is familiar. "The great principles of the State", the great convert wrote in his lecture on *Certain Difficulties Felt by Anglicans* (1850), "are those of the Church, and, if the State would but keep within its own province, it would find the Church its

truest ally and best benefactor." Why? Because the Church "upholds
obedience to the magistrate; she recognises his office as from God;
she is the preacher of peace, the sanction of law, the first element of
order, and the safeguard of morality, and that without possible vacil-
lation or failure; she may be fully trusted; she is a sure friend, for she
is indefectible and undying." The problem, however, as Father Rutler
understands so clearly, is that the usurpatory State will not confine
itself to its proper limits. As Cardinal Newman observed, "it is not
enough for the State that things should be done, unless it has the doing
of them itself; it abhors a double jurisdiction, and what it calls a divided allegiance; *aut Caesar aut nullus*, is its motto, nor does it willingly
accept of any compromise. All power is founded, as it is often said, on
public opinion; for the State to allow the existence of a collateral and
rival authority, is to weaken its own."

And this nicely explains the inordinate interest that the State cur-
rently takes in abortion and other transgressions against the moral law.
It takes this interest, not because it has any solicitude for the well-being
of unborn children or homosexuals, but because it knows that by taking the stance it takes it can aggrandize its own power and undermine
that of the Church. Of course, this epitomizes a certain type of humbug, at which the progressive servants of the State are such shameless
masters. Yet, in essay after essay in this wonderful collection, Father
Rutler exposes the impostures of these and other public men in order
to commend the truths of the Redeemer, convinced, as Saint Bernard
of Clairvaux was convinced, that "What we love we shall grow to resemble."

For example, in one piece here, entitled "Speaking Well of the
Dead", Father Rutler remonstrates with those who chose to eulogize
Justice William J. Brennan in a way that blatantly falsified the legacy
of the man who crafted the legal argument of *Roe v. Wade*. Here, there
is a Johnsonian gravity to Father Rutler's writing, which puts this collection in an entirely different league from the usual run of essays.

The noble pagans flattered their dead because they could not absolve
them. *De mortuis nil nisi bonum* is not a Christian dictum; speaking
nothing but good of the dead bespeaks the Spartan decency of Chilon,
who lived six centuries before the Incarnation of the Redeemer. Chilon
may have been a wise magistrate himself and as merciful as a Spartan

could be, but his mercy was not that of Christ the Judge, for Chilon had no power to summon the dead: "Come forth!" The noble pagan tried to make the best of a bad thing by recommending a social convention born of pessimism. The mercy of God changes pessimism to hope, and hope is the engine of honesty.

This, by any chalk, is good writing. When I said that it reminded me of Johnson's work, I was thinking primarily of the great moralist's *Rambler* essays, though I could easily have cited something that Boswell once said of Johnson, which also describes the essayist in Father Rutler: "His superiority over other learned men consisted chiefly in what may be called the art of thinking, the art of using his mind; a certain continual power of seizing the useful substance of all that he knew, and exhibiting it in a clear and forcible manner; so that knowledge, which we often see to be no better than lumber in men of dull understanding, was, in him, true, evident, and actual wisdom."

A good deal of Father Rutler's wisdom is evident in his altogether salutary criticism of the extent to which his co-religionists have betrayed the obligations of their Catholic faith, especially in relation to the deeply anti-Catholic culture of the now tentacular State. In page after page of this collection, readers will see that this is one Catholic clergyman who does not have his head plunged in the sand when it comes to the consequences of Catholics refusing to defend the moral teachings of the Church. In an essay entitled "Laughing with Caesar", Father Rutler could not be clearer about the nature of this dereliction of duty. "We can dance to Caesar's intolerable music, but he will call the tune. We can feast with Caesar, but he will soon feast on us. We can laugh with Caesar but he will soon laugh at us. *Risus abundat in ore stultorum*. There is abundant laughter in the mouth of the foolish."

Another distinction of these essays is their charm. Evelyn Waugh, in the opening to his great comic novel *The Ordeal of Gilbert Pinfold* (which he based on one of his more traumatic vacations), praised authors who, as he said, exhibited "so much will and so much ability to please". Certainly, in his account of his own vacations, Father Rutler shows how he possesses that will and that ability himself *in excelsio*. Waugh wrote some incomparably good travel books, but I do not know that the author of *Labels, Remote People, Ninety-Two Days*, or *Waugh in Abyssinia* ever managed anything funnier than the essay of Father Rutler on the subject. I realize that comparing Father Rutler to Evelyn Waugh, not to mention Samuel Johnson, is high praise. Does the author of these essays that you now hold in your hands deserve to be spoken of in such illustrious company? I should say that he does, though now you must see whether I am right by reading these sprightly essays for yourself.

EDWARD SHORT

Feast of Saint Gregory the Great
September 3, 2014
Astoria, New York

AUTHOR'S NOTE

AUTHORS MAY NOT BE the best judges of their written thoughts, and the role of the critic is to remind them of that. Such advice is not of great help once the deed has been done, but it is gratifying that readers have at least read what was written. In our computer age, their comments come quickly. I have learned a lot from unsolicited opinions, and one hopes that electronic communication might lead to some glimmer of spiritual communion. A communion most intimate took place when the Risen Lord spoke to the men on the Emmaus road. They asked him to stay with them, and when he spoke to them and broke the bread, they united with the Word behind their feeble words. If we pay attention to personalities and events, and even trivialities and controversies, we may find in them ways that the Lord is speaking to us and communicating some sort of message.

My files are somewhat disordered, and so it seemed useful to assemble some of the things I have written either for particular occasions or as mental dalliances, discerning in them the lordly voice of the One who speaks through art and politics and every aspect of daily life, for nothing is outside the economy of God and man: "Nihil humanum mihi alienum est." Wherever that Emmaus road was in fact, it stretches for all of us from the start of our lives to its setting. Those men tried to make sense of the Man who suddenly appeared walking with them. The men walking along the way include not only Cleopas and the one not named, but everyone who breathes, whether perceptive or obtuse, for that other man may be our surrogate. If the human race is too dull to recognize Christ on those occasions when he appears in the events of each day and in curiosities we stumble upon, he patiently explains to us who are "slow of heart" what is going on.

In selecting some of the essays I have written mostly in recent years, I have drawn from the overly large pile some that address a variety of subjects. Winston Churchill complained at a dinner that the pudding had no theme. Publishers often shy from anthologies for the same reason. The essays I have chosen cover a range of subjects that may seem unrelated and even eclectic, and the serious reader may find some unsettling whimsy creeping in. All that I write is written as a parish priest, and I am happy that is all I have ever been, and so I have had the privilege of being edified by souls in the daily traffic of their lives. If various passages in my essays are pedestrian, my one defense is that the men on the Emmaus road were pedestrians and the Man who walked with them was kind enough to explain that he had planned each step they were taking.

And they said to one another, Were not our hearts burning within us when he spoke to us on the road, and when he made the Scriptures plain to us?

—Luke 24:32

I

THE TRANSFIGURATION OF THE CHURCH

Y EARS AGO, an Oxford don, not rare as an eccentric but singular
in his way of being one, kept in his rooms a small menagerie
including a mongoose, to whom he fed mice for tea, and an eagle
that flew one day into the cathedral and tried to mate with the brass
eagle-shaped lectern, which was cold and unresponsive. It is claimed
that the choristers at that moment were singing "O for the Wings of
a Dove", by Mendelssohn, who had recently dedicated his "Scottish"
Symphony to Queen Victoria. No dove is safe around an eagle, and
the dove and the eagle represent in iconography very different aspects
of the spiritual life. The oldest eagle lectern in Oxford is not in the
cathedral but in nearby Corpus Christi college chapel, and there are
eagle lecterns all over the world, symbolizing Saint John, whose record
of the saving Gospel soars on wings not of this world.

Curious it is, then, that Saint John is the only evangelist who does
not record the ethereal mystery of the Transfiguration, and especially
so since he was there: "We have beheld his glory, glory as of the only-
begotten Son from the Father" (1:14). Some of the mystical writers
explain that the entire Fourth Gospel is one long and radiant transfiguration. If the event is a lacuna for John, he makes up for it by being the
only evangelist to record the marriage at Cana, which in some ways is a
prototype of the Transfiguration. Before both events, Jesus had assured
his apostles that they would see a great glory, and on both occasions
he spoke of an approaching hour that was his destiny. "This, the first

Originally published in *Crisis Magazine*, March 12, 2013.

of his signs, Jesus did at Cana in Galilee, and manifested his glory; and his disciples believed in him" (Jn 2:11).

In a sort of yin-yang contrast, the wedding miracle is soon followed by the violent cleansing of the Temple, just as the Transfiguration leads to a wild encounter at the foot of the mountain with an epileptic. A Russian proverb holds that when the Lord builds a church, Satan pitches a tent across the street. The endless agony of Lucifer without the Light is that he cannot get far enough away from the eternal brightness, and yet he is helplessly drawn to it, like an ugly moth to a lovely flame. There is some of that tension in those who talk incessantly about why they will have nothing to do with the Church. A Christ who does not inspire will seem to haunt. But only ghosts haunt, and Christ is not a ghost, for a ghost does not have flesh and bones as he has. This strange obsession is from a darker source.

The Church Militant, which in its weakest moments may seem like a scattered and tattered regiment of the Church Triumphant, has supernal guarantees that the gates of hell shall not prevail against it. Any reformation of the Church that is not a transfiguration by the light of that confidence becomes a deformation. With the best intentions, sectaries spring up to fix the cracks they see in the Rock which is Peter, using some principle other than his power to bind and loose. This is not to impugn the moral protocols of those denominations, which often excel the practice of Catholics. Ronald Knox observed, and almost boasted, that only Catholic churches had signs saying, "Mind your umbrella." But the Catholic Church, by being Catholic, cannot succumb to polemic, for she is not founded on any theory, and when the Antichrist attacks in ways carnal or psychological, his battering rams only bolster the barricades. Sinners in the Church's ranks sin most easily when times are easy, while martyrs, apologists, and doctors flourish best in the worst times.

Christ's glory filled the sky as he predicted his death in order to strengthen his disciples for the time when the sky would be darkened. Peter wanted to stay on top of Mount Tabor in its afterglow, like a fly in amber. Christ had more in mind: not nostalgia, but tradition, which passes the glory on to the disciples, filling them "with all the fulness of God" (Eph 3:19). Nostalgia is the climate of Quietism, the anemic spirituality that basks in God's goodness without doing anything about it. It does not go down from Tabor to go up to Jerusalem. It inverts the Christian life by being of the world but not in it. This is religion as a virtue turned into religiosity as a vice, confusing grace with uncompromising rectitude and sanctification with unrelenting perfectionism. The perfectionist wants to be good, and that is a subtle blasphemy: "Why do you ask me about what is good? One there is who is good. If you would enter life, keep the commandments" (Mt 19:17). This same Christ, who cannot contradict himself, had already said: "You, therefore, must be perfect, as your heavenly Father is perfect" (Mt 5:48). Goodness is from within, while perfection is from without. The perfectionist wants to make himself good, better, and best. But the Perfect Man said, "apart from me you can do nothing" (Jn 15:5). That is why he gave us the Church as his Body and, by so doing, saves mortal man from the degradation of trying to feel good about himself.

Perfectionists are easily scandalized by what is not good. Saints are only scandalized by what is not glorious. We may say in cliché "Nobody's perfect", but the fact is, saints are perfect, and they are precisely so because they do not try to be good, better, and best. The more they are transfigured by the Light, the more they seem to themselves bad, worse, and worst. Perfectionists resent the weaknesses of which saints boast: "My grace is sufficient for you, for my power is made perfect in weakness" (2 Cor 12:9). The perfectionist misses this whole point, and so, like the narrow kind of Pharisee, he casts a cold eye on the failings of humans, as if the failings abolish the humanity. The saints, having seen the glory on the mountaintop, do not gaze at themselves but "see only Jesus", who, rather than transforming them into goodness, transfigures them into glory. From his own lofty height, Saint Maximos the Confessor could say, "All that God is, except for an identity of being, one becomes when one is deified by grace." And he was not the first to say it. Peter, who wanted to tarry on the mountain, would soon enough be speaking of "precious promises" by which "you may . . . become partakers of the divine nature" (2 Pet 1:4).

In clumsy hands this language would become superhuman rather than supernatural. Under wrong impressions and bereft of inspiration, the Mormon version thinks it means becoming another god with a personal planet. This requires a heavy editing of the Word of God. A "Bible Dictionary" of the Latter Day Saints notes that "the Cambridge University Press granted the Church permission to use its Bible dictionary as a base, to be amended as needed." In that editing, the Mormon dictionary says of the Transfiguration: "Few events in the Bible equal it in importance. A similar event occurred on April 3, 1836, in the temple at Kirtland, Ohio, where the same heavenly messengers conferred priesthood keys upon the Prophet Joseph Smith and Oliver Cowdery." Unconvinced as I am of this, I am persuaded that the Transfiguration illuminates the salutary crisis of the Holy Catholic Church in our time, with Christ flanked by Moses and Elijah, shedding light on law and learning.

In his last Angelus address, Benedict XVI said that he is now going up the mountain as did Peter, James, and John, and there he will pray. He knows that at the foot of the mountain are all kinds of noise and foaming, and these are the growls of the Prince of Darkness paying the Church a tribute he pays no other reality: his hatred. While he mocks men and scorns their pretensions, he reserves his bitterness for the Church, which is the only thing he fears in this world. His backhanded compliment is the distress, gossip, and corruption he sows among the disciples. This is why dissent within the Church can be far more raucous than assaults from without. Those who have never discovered Catholicism are not as caustic in their disdain as are those who claim to be recovering from it. Georges Bernanos said, "We do not lose our faith. We simply stop shaping our lives by it." The life that has lost its shape can be more destructive than the life that was not shaped at all, and this accounts for the "recovering Catholics" who are more bitter about why the Church is wrong than those who never thought the Church was right to begin with. Those who knew not what they were doing were forgiven from the Cross, while the man who knew what he was doing hanged himself. The same Paul who told the Athenians that God overlooked their ignorance of the Gospel cursed those who twisted the Gospel (cf. Acts 17:30; Gal 1:9). Christ can be double-crossed only by those who once were marked with his Cross.

When things seem especially confused in the Church and scandals abound, that is a hint from heaven and a murmur from hell that something profoundly blessed is about to happen. Christ prays for Peter when the devil tries to sift him like wheat, so that when Peter survives, he will confirm the brethren in a lively tradition of glory "We did not follow cleverly devised myths when we made known to you the power and coming of our Lord Jesus Christ, but we were eyewitnesses of his majesty. . . . We heard this voice borne from heaven, for we were with him on the holy mountain" (2 Pet 1:16–18).

2

THE AWKWARDNESS OF ADVENT

T HE STAR that Jean-Paul Sartre once was, doyen of his day's in-completely educated intellectuals, has not quietly faded the way splashy names often do in the generation after they die. His star has astonishingly imploded. Some echoes remain, for he was not devoid of a way with words, nor was he without rays of light seeping through his melancholy philosophy. George Will remarked once that "Sartre looks like a man who got bad news in 1947 and still hasn't gotten over it." Even if his existentialism did not include belief in the existence of hell, he described its nonexistence well as the place where you have nothing to do but amuse yourself. That was before a new crop of peo-ple appeared, Twittering in solitude surrounded by crowds. It was not before people began making Christmas hellish by trying to celebrate a "joy without a cause". That phrase from Chesterton's *The Ballad of the White Horse* was published in 1911, but two years earlier in *All Things Considered* he was quite specific: "There is no more dangerous or disgusting habit than that of celebrating Christmas before it comes."

Not to patronize them, it may be that those who light up Christ-mas trees in November are sending a frail signal that they do not want to be numbered among the people who "loved darkness rather than light" (Jn 3:19). Perhaps even more poignantly, those who are hostile to Christmas and would ban its very mention by so doing betray an uneasy suspicion that an Incarnation might be of more than moral in-terest and could even have cosmic implications if it really happened, puncturing the numbness of their sense of life.

Originally published in *Crisis Magazine*, December 6, 2012.

The grammatical construction called "apophasis", which is saying what will not be said, works nicely here: it is futile to say that we should not trample over Advent in the rush to Christmas. It is even pointless to point out the inappropriateness of poinsettias around cathedral altars starting after Thanksgiving ("because the tourists expect that") and avuncular clergymen hosting children's Christmas parties before Gaudete Sunday. Advent is awkward because its mysteries of death, judgment, heaven, and hell are not the sort of things countertenors dressed as elves sing about. As Saint Paul wrote in his Epistle to the New Yorkers: "Fuhgeddaboudit."

In the four weeks of Advent, the Church stops us from skimming on the surface of reality: eating, working, shopping, sleeping, waking up, and doing it all over again. These are part of the dance of life, but they are not its sum. "Angst" is a neurosis stemming from an unwillingness to face the Choreographer behind the choreography. Those threadbare philosophers who made existence an "ism" were very anxious indeed, smoking their cigarettes in cafes across the street from vacant churches.

A culture trapped in its own existence becomes no greater than itself. That old maxim perdures no matter how many times it is repeated: "A man wrapped up in himself becomes a very small package." More important than wrapping gifts in Advent is the obligation to unwrap the self: to confess to Christ the sins that belittle his image in man and to live life as he wants it, so that we might rejoice with him forever and never be separated from him.

Our culture is enduring a severe test of itself. If Christ does not govern minds and hearts, mere humans will volunteer to do it, and they will do it badly. When the Judges of Israel could think about their own existence only with reference to how other people existed apart from divine regiment, they wanted a human king. Samuel warned them: "He will take the best of your fields and vineyards and olive orchards and give them to his servants. . . . He will take the tenth of your flocks, and you shall be his slaves" (1 Sam 8:14, 17). These days, he will take a lot more than 10 percent.

Our Lord promises that the truth will set us free: not truths, but truth, and that truth is himself. In him is the explanation of death, judgment, heaven, and hell. All facts physical and moral issue from him who "is before all things, and in him all things hold together" (Col 1:17). The "holy grail" of physics, a Unified Theory of the Universe, may not be attainable; but Einstein's close friend John Wheeler, of Johns Hopkins and Princeton, predicted shortly before he died in 2008 that if it is found, the biggest surprise about it will be its simplicity. Jesus could not have expressed himself more simply when he told Pontius Pilate: "Every one who is of the truth hears my voice" (Jn 18:37). Pilate's life in a backwater of the empire was a dreary routine mired in cynicism. But even Pilate was amazed that Christ's own people had "handed him over" to the government. By their own declaration when Pilate took a poll of them, they wanted "no king but Caesar". Each generation is tempted to hand Christ over to cynics. We do it when we barter our conscience for comfort and our freedom for frivolity.

If Catholics behaved as Catholics, living as Catholics in their homes and voting as Catholics in the public forum, our culture would not indulge a precarious tranquility, content with getting little things from elected officials in exchange for moral dignity. If we only want things, we shall only be things. Amid the passing fashions of mindless men, Christ says, "You will be brought before kings and governors for my name's sake. This will be a time for you to bear testimony" (Lk 21:12–13).

Advent is a time for such testimony. However many Advents we may be allowed to have, the last one will be the one for which all other Advents prepared. Even Jean-Paul Sartre seems to have glimpsed that, for as death approached he began to speak of some sort of Messianic Judaism. Later, his mistress, Simone de Beauvoir, acidly called it "this senile act of a turncoat". In a testimony recorded by his friend and former Marxist Pierre Victor, Sartre said: "I do not feel that I am the product of chance, a speck of dust in the universe, but someone who was expected, prepared, prefigured. In short, a being whom only a Creator could put here; and this idea of a creating hand refers to God."

It would be difficult to think of anyone more unlike Sartre than his contemporary political philosopher Charles Maurras, who recovered his Catholic faith only late in life. In Sartre's better moments, in the Second World War, he resisted the barbarism with which Maurras cooperated. But each had his last Advent. Sartre's last words were, "I have failed." As for Maurras, who had become deaf as a teenager, he said to the doctor at his bedside: "At last I can hear someone coming."

3

REJOICE, JERUSALEM

I T IS IRONIC that the scintillating Graeco-Syrian Saint Luke was martyred, according to tradition, in Boeotia, a humid and swampy part
of central Greece whose people were said to be not interested in philosophy or much of anything beyond their uneventful daily lives. That
may have been the propaganda of the superior Athenians, who carica-
tured the Boeotians and indeed anyone not Athenian, the way some
Irish make Kerrymen the butt of jokes. The great Pindar was Boeotian, but for the most part the fetid place was not considered a nursery
of genius, and the Boeotians remained the equivalent of people today
whose cultural universe is confined to watching ESPN. The Romans
absorbed the Greek prejudice and had an expression: "Boeotum in
crasso jurares aere natum"—"You'd swear he was born in the thick
air of Boeotia."

If Luke died in Boeotia, he certainly was not Boeotian in outlook.
He traveled widely and observed his world with an artist's eye. As
Horace compared poetry with painting, so did Luke make word pictures of historical sketches, adding the immediacy of a reporter; for if
the Good News is new, it needs a news reporter. Luke accompanied
Paul, who mentions him in his letters to Philemon, Timothy, and the
Colossians. His vivid Acts of the Apostles paints psychological por-
traits in a rupture from the stylized forms of what had long passed for
narrative history in the classical world. In one scene he records how
some of the people of Thessalonica objected to what Paul and Silas
had been preaching. The two had found shelter in the house of Jason

Originally published in *Crisis Magazine*, December 14, 2012.

and seem to have fled the mob. Jason and some of his fellows were dragged before the public officials and were accused: "These men who have turned the world upside down have come here also . . . and they are all acting against the decrees of Caesar, saying that there is another king, Jesus" (Acts 17:6–7). It is a brilliant anticipation of what is said in our own secular culture as Christianity is proscribed as politically incorrect. In the next chapter, Luke describes Paul on trial before Lucius Junius Gallio Annaeus, proconsul of Achaia. Gallio, representing the best in Roman jurisprudence, threw out the case brought against Paul because it had nothing to do with Roman civil law. Gallio was the brother of the most revered Stoic philosopher, Lucius Annaeus Seneca. Like Paul, the two brothers would die under Nero, in their cases by forced suicide.

Stoicism was a grin-and-bear-it philosophy: there is no point in expecting happiness in a future life, since a soul if immortal lacks eternal individuality and will be absorbed into a "cosmic wholeness". The only happiness consists in the satisfaction of cultivating the natural virtues. With pliable rectitude, the Stoics did not perfectly practice what they preached, overlapping somewhat with the Epicureans, and Seneca indulged in a luxurious life himself. They did pride themselves on moral discipline, with a consequent stiff-upper-lip attitude to suffering. Seneca taught that if you feared losing something, practice doing without it while you had it. So, for instance, if you feared losing comforts, "set aside a certain number of days, during which you shall be content with the scantiest and cheapest fare, with coarse and rough dress, saying to yourself the while: 'This is the condition that I feared.'" They called this "the premeditation of evils".

Some mistakenly have thought that Paul exchanged letters with Seneca and was something of a Stoic himself. He does say: "We rejoice in our sufferings, knowing that suffering produces endurance" (Rom 5:3), but, unlike the Stoics, he believed that hardships and spiritual disciplines shouldered uncomplainingly prepare the soul for the joys of heaven. So on Gaudete Sunday in penitential Advent, a little unearthly light seeps into earthly darkness, and the Church chants: "Rejoice in the Lord always; again I will say, Rejoice. Let all men know your forbearance. The Lord is at hand. Have no anxiety about anything, but in everything by prayer and supplication with thanksgiving let your requests be made known to God" (Phil 4:4–6).

Governments, kings, and rulers of all sorts come and go, and when they are good, their passing from this mortal coil engenders sadness, and when they are evil, their end makes their survivors happy, at least for awhile. Joy, however, never ends, for it is fealty to Christ whose kingdom is not of this world. By coming "to his own", he sets the world aright, and only those who have been accustomed to an upside-down world think that he has upset it. That is the same disordered perspective that thinks holiness is insane and sin is sane.

It is characteristic of people who think that disorder is natural that they are given to sadness. Calvinism, like the ancient Stoicism, was of that hue, thinking of life as making the best of a bad thing. This was expressed in the film *The African Queen* by Katharine Hepburn's character, Rose Sayer, a Methodist missionary in German East Africa who unctuously explains: "Nature is what we were put on earth to rise above." There is more than a dash of that in the Jansenism that weaves its way in and out of various Catholic enthusiasms. They claim to be of the sacred tradition but distort the apostolic faith to the extent of giving the impression that the Word was made flesh and dwelt among us in order to make people dress modestly. The common characteristic of those who, in the words of the nineteenth-century Archbishop De Péréfix of Paris, are "pure as angels, but as proud as devils" is a lack of joy. C. S. Lewis absorbed some of that mentality in the culture of Ulster, and when he finally embraced a radiant Christianity, he was "surprised by joy". The Catholic saints are never surprised by joy, because they are only surprised by a lack of it in the world around them. Just as Christ was transfigured and not transformed, so Aquinas teaches, contrary to Rose Sayer, that grace does not destroy nature but perfects it. "Jerusalem gaude. Rejoice, Jerusalem." If our little rejoicings come off as gaudy tinsel, they are furtive sparks from that Light which enlightens every man. As man is in the image of God, human nature can come fully alive only by reflecting that Light: "Then our mouth was filled with laughter, and our tongue with shouts of joy . . . The LORD has done great things for us; we are glad" (Ps 126:2). For all their admirable traits, the Stoics disdained those who were happy because they were happy. They were like the sober skeptics of our own time who think, like the somber Oxford philosopher who studied the subject thoroughly, that happiness is no laughing matter. In response, the Church keeps laughing, dresses gaudily, and sings, "Rejoice, Jerusalem."

4

ON LETTING THE LIGHT SHINE

A S A RATHER OBSERVANT CHILD, I made a mental note of the fact
that my maternal grandmother would ask me to "make a light"
instead of asking me to switch it on. When she was a child, no one
switched lights on. At night, light was not had without effort, not in
her English town nor in most places yet. She was born on the day
that Gladstone introduced his Irish Home Rule bill in the House of
Commons, the same Gladstone who gave a lamp to Newman, who
had never "sinned against the light", a lamp that still can be seen on his
desk in Birmingham, and it certainly was not electric. Four years after
my grandmother's birth, Florence Nightingale recorded her voice on a
wax cylinder patented by the Edison Company. My grandmother harbored a devotion to the "Lady with a Lamp", for her town's regiment
had fought in the Crimean War, and some of them remembered the
Lady visiting at night the wards in the Selimiye Barracks of Scutari, and
it most definitely was not an electric lamp: that was the year Thomas
Edison was born.

While eclectic in theology, and something of a Universalist, Florence
Nightingale moved from Unitarianism to Anglicanism and soon came
to admire the slum work of the future Cardinal Manning, who provided
her with ten Catholic nuns to help nurse the soldiers in the war. They,
along with fourteen Anglican nuns, nurtured the English custom of
calling all nurses, mostly secular but usually veiled, "Sister". A lamp,
not electric, became the symbol of nursing organizations even in the

Originally published in *Crisis Magazine*, February 7, 2014.

United States. Then there was the friend of my grandmother, a very old lady, Granny Pye as I called her, who had been born in Scotland in the year that the missionary David Livingston died in Zambia. Although she belonged to the Old Kirk that did not allow ritual candles, she had a ritual of her own, for she read from the family Bible every night by candlelight, as though light bulbs were somewhat profane.

My point is that artificial light is so available now, at the flip of a switch, that we are losing a sense of wonder at the gift of light. The first creature was light itself: "Let there be light." It is hard to describe light without referring to its opposite. "The people who walked in darkness have seen a great light" (Is 9:2). The first thing one learns in painting, after tackling perspective, is that colors seem bright only by contrast, and that principle of chiaroscuro was known well before the likes of Caravaggio and de la Tour. You do not have to spend a winter in Lapland to know that: just spend a few dim days in February, or try selling an apartment without a view.

Light and life go together, and there are countless "last words" that have to do with light as life ends. It is said that, as he was dying, Goethe cried out, "Mehr Licht!—More light!" but in his case it probably had no spiritual meaning. He had also been a scientist who considered his best book to be *The Theory of Colors*. He most likely was just asking that the shutters be opened. To give him his due, anyone who has read his *Faust* knows that he also knew of moral darkness and what happens in chambers of the mind that choose darkness over light. In retrospect, it is poignant, though not of any religious significance, that Theodore Roosevelt said as he went to bed for the last time: "Please put out the light." He was thinking of electricity and not mortality. That good man just wanted a good sleep, but he did not know how good it would be. Very different and far from prosaic was what young O. Henry, abandoned by his wife, Sara, said with his last alcoholic breath in the dim gaslight of his rented room: "Turn up the lights— I don't want to go home in the dark." However oblique his spiritual intuition may have been, it seems laden with an ancient appeal to One "in [whom] is no darkness at all" (1 Jn 1:5).

Our Lord's utterances stunned, enthralled, and shocked the crowds, but none was more startling than this: "I am the light of the world; he who follows me will not walk in darkness, but will have the light of life" (Jn 8:12). As the light itself, his human decibels shouted to the sky that his essence was not a creature but the Divinity, who creates physical light with the agency of "the Father of lights with whom there is no variation or shadow due to change" (Jas 1:17) and who, with their Spirit, will "enlighten the hearts of the faithful" with the fire of love. Frail human voices have the inestimable privilege of professing that mystery each Sunday in the Creed: Jesus of Nazareth is "Light from Light" from beyond Nazareth.

God offers the human race the light of life in order that it might "shine before men, that they may see your good works and give glory to your Father who is in heaven" (Mt 5:16). Morally, the exercise of free will can make that light beautiful or garish. On his visit to the United States that gave the world so many congenial quotes, G. K. Chesterton was entranced by the billboard lights in Times Square advertising soaps and cigarettes and hair tonic: "What a garden of delights this place would be for anyone who couldn't read."

Our Lord dignifies the human race by enabling his own light to shine through his human creatures so that it might give "light to all in the house" (Mt 5:15). That house includes everyone's own neighborhood, with its astonishing challenges and potential. In my own instance, that neighborhood, which is my parish, consists right now in the largest real estate development in the nation, besides some venerable older fixtures, including the Empire State Building. It becomes a nightly light show of colors that would have got another book out of Goethe. The saints are an even more wonderful light show themselves. They are the "generation of those who seek him" (Ps 24:6). To risk the rhetorical indecency of a pun, the generator that lights this generation up is not in Manhattan, for it is in the City that "has no need of sun or moon to shine upon it, for the glory of God is its light, and its lamp is the Lamb" (Rev 21:23).

5

INFANDUM

I N 1789 George Washington prayed in Saint Paul's Church, on what
we now call lower Broadway, on the day of his inauguration as the
first president of the United States. The churchyard was already old.
On September 11, 2001, several new corpses were lying on the old
graves. Then quickly a temporary morgue was set up in a nearby hotel.
All that the founding fathers stood for was contradicted in a thunderous attack on the heart of the city that calls itself the capital of the
world.

Grown children had become accustomed to taking prosperity for
granted and had often scorned the virtues that created the prosperity.
The frenzied celebrations of the third millennium were largely conspicuous for their cheerful banality. There were fireworks but no great
blazing works of art. A generation after men went to the moon, cele-
brants did circles on Ferris wheels; in London a dome was built with
no particular purpose in mind and was hastily filled with just about
everything except an altar to God. The general euphoria was tinged
with melancholy, almost like that of Alexander with no more worlds
to conquer. What to do with endless peace? Some said that history had
ended. Then came an airplane flying so low, in a city that usually does
not notice noise of any kind, that I had to take notice.

Crowds screamed and ran when the first tower fell; when the second
came down, many just sat stupefied on the ground and groaned. Those
buildings were not widely loved by New Yorkers. In the 1960s when

Originally published in *Crisis Magazine*, November 1, 2001.

Penn Station was dismantled, they were built with the rebarbative euphoria of the "International School", whose architects and sycophantic political backers defied everything that had gone before. An architect famously complained that the towers "tilted" the Manhattan skyline.

They stood, nonetheless, tall evangels of great enterprise, and at night when their cold steel was a shadow and their lights flooded the harbor, they could stun sullen eyes. Those who saw them collapse felt a collapse in themselves. About 25 percent of the onlookers are said to have had post-traumatic stress, a syndrome that can be traced back to the silence of our first ancestors as they left Eden in shock. Helpless reporters, kept at a distance, heard from eyewitnesses responses like that of Aeneas when Dido asked him to recount the loss of his ships and sailors: "Infandum, regina, iubes renovare dolorem" (O queen, you bid me retell a tale that should not be uttered).

The horrific shock treatment of September 11 has rattled three modern assumptions. The first was the politicized dismissal of natural law. George Washington in his pew at Saint Paul's believed in the inalienable right to life. The primacy of natural law was vindicated when people at the World Trade Center struggled to rescue one another, often sacrificing their lives to do so. A man leaving his apartment to go to work in one of the towers heard his wife crying that she was going into labor. Instead of going to his office, he took her to the hospital and watched his baby enter the world as his building collapsed. The baby's first act was to save his father. In a world of carnage in Bethlehem, men once heard the cry of the baby who saves all those who call upon him, through all ages, even as late as September 11, 2001. The thousands of lives crushed on that day will make it harder to say that life does not count.

Secondly, the holy priesthood has been a victim of modern assault. God's gift of priestly intercession has recently become an object of incomprehension and mockery. Books were written on how the priesthood might be reformed out of existence. A saint once said that a priest is a man who would die to be one. On September 11, a chaplain of the New York City Fire Department was crushed while giving the last rites to a dying fireman. Members of his company carried him to New York's oldest Catholic church a few blocks away and laid him on the marble pavement in front of the altar. Each knelt at the altar rail before going back to the flames. I stayed a while and saw the blood flow down the altar steps. Above the altar was a painting of Christ bleeding on the Cross—the gift of a Spanish king and old enough for Saint Elizabeth Ann Seton to have prayed before it. More than local Catholic history was encompassed in that scene. For those who had forgotten, the Eucharist is a sacrifice of blood, and it is the priest who offers the sacrifice. September 11 gave an indulgent world, and even delicate catechists, an icon of the priesthood.

The fall of the towers quaked modern man's third error: his contempt for objective truth. The whole world said that what happened on September 11 was hideously wrong, and suddenly we realized how rarely in recent times we have heard things that are hideous and wrong *called* hideous and wrong. So many firemen wanted to confess before entering the chaos that we priests gave general absolution. They would not have wanted to confess if they had not known the portent of the moment; nor would they have made the sign of the cross if they had thought existence was a jumbled quilt of inconsequential opinions. A rescue worker next to me boasted that his lucky penny and his little crucifix had saved him when he was tossed ten feet in the air by the reverberations of falling steel. He got up, brushed himself off, and went back into the bedlam. If he was superstitious, he was only half so. Pope John Paul II has often been patronized by savants who thought that his description of a "culture of death" was extravagantly romantic pessimism. They have not spoken like that since September 11.

A crowd of people blinded by smoke were panicking in a Wall Street subway exit. One man calmly led them to safety. He was blind, and he and his seeing-eye dog knew every corner of that station. One might say—and if one were rational, one would have to say—that each generation, culturally blinded in ways peculiar to its age, is offered a hand to safety by people whose holiness is often considered a handicap. At the World Trade Center, rescued men and women were heard to use words like "guardian angel" and "savior". Days later, confession lines were long and congregations stood in the streets outside packed churches. One waits to see if grace will build upon grace.

Perhaps it would be naïve to hope that a new Christian consciousness suddenly and smoothly will arise. On a train a few days after the attack, I sat next to a teenager wearing the ritual garb of his atomistic tribe, backwards baseball cap and such. When I recounted how rescuers had kept rushing into 240,000 tons of collapsing ironwork without any apparent thought for themselves, he replied in a voice coached by the sentinels of self-absorption: "They must be sick." It will take more than one September day to humanize a generation.

We were attacked on what was to have been the day of the primary elections for the city's mayoral office. One policeman, speaking through a gas mask, gasped how all this chaos made all those candidates and all their "issues" seem so small. (That is only the gist of what he said; he used sturdy monosyllabic Tudor metaphors appropriate to the passion of the moment.) I do not see that problem being quickly cured. William Clinton, still unaccustomed to his reduced place in life, arrived on the scene the day before the president. The spectacle of his pumping up oceans of empathy in front of cameras carried bad taste to a length he had not managed even in the White House. Sobered by the day's events, the media virtually ignored him. As a chronicler said of Napoleon, "He embarrassed God." Within days, an organist from another state faxed offers of special fees to parishes whose organists could not manage the number of funerals. A company from Maine advertised handheld devices that send sonic vibrations to soothe grief.

Such inanities of the human race can only be understood as little burps from Beelzebub's inferior minions. Beelzebub did not win the day against courage. In a World War II speech, Churchill paraphrased Saint Thomas Aquinas in describing courage as the foundational quality for all the virtues. The politicians of his day who wanted compromise with evil do not share a place on his plinth, and nations that were neutral then do not boast of it now. When asked about evacuating Elizabeth and Margaret Rose during the blitz, Queen Elizabeth famously said that the princesses "will not leave unless I leave, and I will not leave unless the King leaves, and the King will not leave." On September 11, through the roaring and crashing and screaming, it may be that many began to hear Christ the King as if for the first time: "I am with you always, to the close of the age."

6

ANGER MANAGEMENT

E ACH GENERATION typically imposes a blanket condemnation of the previous one out of impatience with the flaws that youth sees in the aged. This impatience is animated by a sense of superiority that, if unfounded in fact, is what C. S. Lewis called "chronological arrogance". Within the many fine phrases that embroider the confidence of the Second Vatican Council, especially in the Pastoral Constitution on the Church in the Modern World, *Gaudium et Spes*, there is a bit of that, in the assumption that the dawn with all its perils will be rosy. In a commentary in 1969, the future Benedict XVI called its account of free will "downright Pelagian" and never mentioned it in his own encyclical on hope, *Spe Salvi*. Chronological arrogance can also be sublimated in pious forms of detraction, such as apologizing for the crimes of people long dead. *Aggiornamento* can be the innocent flexing of youthful vigor, but it can also be the naïve chanting of babes in the wood.

The "Angry Young Men" of Britain in the 1950s were a rather vague assortment of writers who had survived a world war only to find themselves in a struggle of a more subtle moral dimension in which their imagined benign future was being held back by calcified social conventions. While they were right in contending that the age's miseries had been brought about by old prejudices and sheer stupidity, they forgot that the defeat of Axis brutality was the result of the heroism produced by the same culture they disparaged. One angry young man was

Originally published in *Crisis Magazine*, August 21, 2012.

John Osborne, author of *Look Back in Anger*, and another was Kingsley Amis, who wrote *Lucky Jim* and later was honest enough to forswear the Communism of his youthful idealism.

At least they were vital enough to be angry. We now inhabit a hedonistic culture too slothful to be angry about much of anything, which is why it is easily bought off by sensual gratifications of the crudest sorts. Where there is anger in the Church, it tends to reverse what angered the previous generation. That is to say, the parents and grandparents of today's young people showed their gratuitous spite by demolishing the sacred traditions. Now the reaction is against that reaction, and churches are being restored, Gregorian chant is bidding guitars goodbye, and nuns riding around on buses to relive their Kumbaya days are indulged with a strained politeness reserved for slightly dotty great aunties. Untamed, this new anger can be as problematic as what angers it. While a classical revival has an inner integrity, the romanticism of some who confect an idealized past that never was is fragile and bound to disappoint, just like the eirenic optimism of the 1960s.

Jesus chose some angry young men to be his apostles, but their anger was not delusional. At least it was a passion that our Lord tamed and directed in the ways of righteousness. James and John were his "Sons of Thunder". Some philologists maintain that their nickname Boanerges, "benē reghesh", really meant that they were, not thunderous, but only windbags. It may even be the case that the blowhard was their mother, Salome. When they wanted to bring lightning down on the Samaritans, they could only imitate the sound of thunder, but real fire was lacking. The Holy Spirit would take that energy and channel it. Anger as a deadly sin is like an oil spill instead of oil for energy. When anger is used rightly, it becomes strength. Satan wants us to lose our temper, but Christ wants us to use it, the only way it should be used: to defeat Satan himself. Saint Paul was not easily tamed, but he would later write in quotation of Psalm 4:4: "Be angry but do not sin; do not let the sun go down on your anger, and give no opportunity to the devil" (Eph 4:26–27). A locomotive may let off steam, but that does not move it. Angry James became the first apostle to offer his life serenely for the Lord, and thundering John in his maturity wrote, "Little children, love one another."

For Christ, sinful anger, the loss of temper, is murderous: "You have heard that it was said to the men of old, 'You shall not kill; and whoever kills shall be liable to judgment.' But I say to you that every one who is angry with his brother shall be liable to judgment; whoever insults his brother shall be liable to the council, and whoever says, 'You fool!' shall be liable to the hell of fire" (Mt 5:21–22). Just as lust is a perversion of love, so Saint Gregory of Nyssa describes anger as a twisting of courage. In the history of social pathology, neurotic people have camouflaged their psychosis in righteous causes. John Brown was a fanatic whose uncontrolled temper made him a mockery of martyrdom, but that did not discredit the abolition movement. The pro-life movement is the noblest cause of our days, and it is not less so for the few mentally disturbed people who wrap themselves in its mantle. Their anger is "of the flesh", but that does not disprove anger that is righteous.

Christ himself is the model of righteous anger. In railing against the hypocrisy of the Pharisees and the venality of the Temple's money changers, he directs it against Satan, who wants man to "lose" his temper by using people and circumstances as distractions to deflect the anger from him. So he plays on human pride, which is the elemental sin that makes anger destructive rather than holy. "A man of wrath stirs up strife, and a man given to anger causes much transgression. A man's pride will bring him low, but he who is lowly in spirit will obtain honor" (Prov 29:22–23).

Righteous anger is like harnessed wind power, while sinful anger is, to use an infelicitous metaphor, just passing wind. The Apostle to the Gentiles warned the Galatians that their uncontrolled temper was a "work of the flesh" (cf. Gal 5:19–23) only after the risen Christ had converted his destructive wrath on the Damascus road. If you are tempted to morose delectation, you should avoid reading Saint Jerome's letters to Saint Augustine, which show how hard it was for him to control his tongue and pen. And as for Saint Columba, a modern dentist might warn him against grinding his teeth.

Now then, there is a problem, and it is this: the notion that the antidote to sinful anger is timidity. No saint, naturally placid or aggressive, makes that mistake. "God did not give us a spirit of timidity but a spirit of power and love and self-control" (2 Tim 1:7). The cure for both kinds of sinfulness, angry and timid, is the virtue of courage. Saint John Chrysostom wrote to Theodore "For if the wrath of God were a passion, one might well despair as being unable to quench the flame which he had kindled by so many evil doings; but since the Divine nature is passionate, even if He punishes, even if He takes vengeance, He does this not with wrath, but with tender care, and much loving-kindness; wherefore it behoves us to be of much courage, and to trust in the power of repentance."[1]

I do not know which is worse: sinful anger, which thinks that it is just, or timidity, which thinks that it is charitable. In our media-conscious culture, timidity easily takes the form of affected joviality, hoping to diffuse tension by amiability: a hug and a slap on the back and then let the "dialogue" begin. That may work with victims of evil but not with the minions of the Evil One himself. Prophecy is not birthed by Hegelian synthesis. During his forty days in the desert, our Lord never joked in the hope of charming the dark and brooding spirit who can only laugh at others and never with them. The soldiers put a funny hat on Christ, but he made it a crown. His benignity destroyed Satan's burlesque. Anyone in a position of moral authority who thinks he might diffuse the tension between good and evil by playing the minstrel only signals his own insecurity. That would be like the Queen of England wearing a Groucho nose at the opening of Parliament. Laughter is a medicine, but it can also be an opiate, and when someone is constantly laughing, there must be a deep disquiet when the lights go out.

Commenting on our Lord's Eucharistic declaration that he is the Bread come down from heaven, Pope Benedict XVI said that Jesus knew exactly what he was doing in addressing the people "to bring the crowd down to earth and mostly to encourage his disciples to make a decision" (Angelus address, August 19, 2012). Saint Paul wanted Timothy to be temperate, but never a man pleaser. Timidity is not charity. It is distraction from danger. On the Titanic, some passengers noticed bits of ice on the deck, so the band played ragtime a little louder. Saint Augustine said, "God does not need my lie." And of course we also have Churchill's definition of timidity incarnate: "An appeaser is one who feeds a crocodile, hoping it will eat him last."

Saint Alphonsus Liguori was not timid when he counseled: "Even when correcting faults, superiors should be kind." But his kindness

---

[1] Saint John Chrysostom, "An Exhortation to Theodore after His Fall", letter 1, in *Nicene and Post-Nicene Fathers*, 1st series, ed. Philip Schaff (Peabody, Mass.: Hendrickson, 1995), 93.

was the engine of his zeal for the first of the seven spiritual works of mercy: to admonish sinners. The confessors and martyrs, ancient and new, had only one kind of anger management therapy: kneeling down and saying, "Bless me Father, for I have sinned." Then they got up and went to work.

7

CHRIST THE GENTLEMAN

K ING CHARLES II said that a gentleman is one who puts those around
him at ease. Even on his deathbed he apologized to the courtiers in
attendance: "I am sorry, gentlemen, for being such an unconscionable
time a-dying." The Society of Friends was a curiosity to him, especially
because one of his admirals, to whom he owed a large debt, had a son
who belonged to it. When William Penn, as a Quaker, would not doff
his hat to the King, he asked, "Friend Charles, why dost thou remove
thy hat?" The King answered, "Friend William, in circumstances such
as these it is customary for only one man to keep his hat on." Some
accounts attribute the line to the King's brother, the Duke of York,
who was only slightly less jolly and bibulous but even more Unquak-
erly Catholic. We do know that from such happy conversations we got
Pennsylvania and Delaware. In 1669, Charles had agreed to profess the
Catholic faith as a provision in the secret Treaty of Dover when the
political temper in England would permit. It is not true that he was a
mere opportunist with respect to religion, for he openly defended his
Catholic brother's right to the throne. All became clear during his long
time a-dying, when he summoned the Benedictine priest Father John
Huddleston to receive him through the earthly gates to the heavenly
ones.

One of the most glowing sections of Newman's lectures on *The Idea
of a University* is his descant on manners: "Hence it is that it is almost
a definition of a gentleman to say that he is one who never inflicts

Originally published in *Crisis Magazine*, May 9, 2012.

pain." But read his lines carefully. The passage is redolent with irony, for the natural gentleman is not of necessity a Christian: "This description is both refined and, as far as it goes, accurate. He is mainly occupied in merely removing the obstacles which hinder the free and unembarrassed action of those about him; and he concurs with their movements rather than takes the initiative himself."

One risks glibness if not irreverence to say that Christ was a gentleman in the natural sense, but the graciousness of his human nature was "hypostatic" with the Source of Grace, and one sign of this was his habit of putting those around him at ease. Julian of Norwich spoke often of this trait refracted in various ways: "Then *our courteous Lord* sheweth himself to the soul cheerfully with glad countenance, with a friendly welcome."

With protocols from the heavenly court, the courtly Christ went to lengths in calming people and caring for their comfort, even finding a grassy place for the crowds to sit before he preached and asking that a girl he raised from the dead be given something to eat. Never did the Lord "lord it over" anyone, and if the occasional hypocrite or unjust judge or weak disciple became nervous in his presence, it was the fault of their guilt, for he never deliberately intimidated or shamed anyone. It was the very benignity of his presence that cracked their self-importance. Once, when a reporter shouted to the 33rd President: "Give 'em hell, Harry!" Truman replied, "I don't give them hell. I just tell the truth about them, and they think it's hell." Our Lord gave people heaven itself, and if that frightened them, it was because their duplicity made heaven hellish.

In the Resurrection, our Lord kept putting people at ease: "Peace." "Do not be afraid." "Why are you troubled?" He let the Magdalene first think he was a gardener, perhaps so that she might not faint, and when he made himself known to the men on the Emmaus road, he may have done it with a smile that stirred hearts slow to believe. He went so far as to let the apostles touch his wounds, and he ate a piece of baked fish to domesticate their incredulity. I expect that the only one our Lord did not have to tell to calm down was our Lady, who was full of grace.

Jesus had no need to apologize for having been such a time a-dying, because instead of inflicting pain, he had taken all the world's pain on himself, and his very agony was a grace. He did another gracious thing by spending the forty days before the Ascension explaining how all the tangled events of history shaped a picture and how the prophets were prophetic. You can tell how well he taught by the way the apostles later wrote their letters, always with that gentle zeal for souls that makes the term "gentleman" inadequate to describe souls so sympathetic. When he had "opened their minds to understand the Scriptures", he told those in the Upper Room to "stay in the city, until you are clothed with power from on high" (Lk 24:45, 49). We know that Peter listened very carefully, for when he was clothed in that elegant spiritual haberdashery which is sanctifying grace, he delicately told the people in Jerusalem that they had acted out of ignorance, but if they repented, the Lord would grant them "times of refreshing", for the Lord, unbending to evil and fierce in the face of the Evil One, is also gentle in all his ways.

8

THE SHORES OF TRIPOLI

I N A FREQUENTLY MISQUOTED LINE from *The Life of Reason*, George San-
tayana said: "Those who cannot remember the past are condemned
to repeat it." Cultural amnesia, helpless or deliberate, does enable people to rewrite history without compunction, and it also makes it easy
for others to believe the fiction as fact or to suppose in a "nunc pro
tunc" way that projects our assumptions onto the ways things were
seen in the past. I should guess that most of our leaders in government
today could not pass the qualifying examination in history that was
required for a high school diploma in the State of New York at the
beginning of the twentieth century. I cite the example of a speech of
President Obama at the fourth annual "Iftar" dinner, a feast at the
end of a day of Ramadan fasting, for assembled Muslims in the White
House on August 10 in this year of 2012:

> As I've noted before, Thomas Jefferson once held a sunset dinner
> here with an envoy from Tunisia—perhaps the first Iftar at the White
> House, more than 200 years ago. And some of you, as you arrived
> tonight, may have seen our special display, courtesy of our friends at
> the Library of Congress—the Koran that belonged to Thomas Jef-
> ferson. And that's a reminder, along with the generations of patriotic
> Muslims in America, that Islam—like so many faiths—is part of our
> national story.

The miscalculation about the role of Muslims in our nation's history
was mentioned previously in President Obama's speech in Cairo on

Originally published in *Crisis Magazine*, September 14, 2012.

June 4, 2009, in which he said he was speaking "as a student of history". As the "Arab Spring" looks increasingly like an autumn headed for winter, it may go in the annals of presidential speeches as the one most tightly packed with mistakes of historical fact: "Islam has always been a part of America's story. The first nation to recognize my country was Morocco. In signing the Treaty of Tripoli in 1796, our second President, John Adams, wrote, 'The United States has in itself no character of enmity against the laws, religion or tranquility of Muslims.' . . . And when the first Muslim-American was recently elected to Congress, he took the oath to defend our Constitution using the same Holy Koran that one of our Founding Fathers—Thomas Jefferson—kept in his personal library."

If I felt confident that President Obama could name some of the Hasmonean kings, I could point out that while they were "a part of the story" of Christianity, they were not so in a positive light. This might put into a better perspective any notion that the Treaty of Tripoli was anything like a free trade agreement or that the Tunisian envoy's dinner with Jefferson was a pleasant interlude or that Jefferson's purchase of "Holy Koran" was part of his quest for oriental wisdom. For one thing, Jefferson's copy was an English translation published in 1734 by George Sale. As it was not in Arabic, it was not any more authentic in the opinion of Muslims than is Farrakhan's "Nation of Islam", which the first Muslim congressman to whom Obama alluded, Keith Ellison, assisted in some of its activities before he abjured it during his election campaign.

In the eighteenth century, Tripoli along with the other Barbary Coast lands of Tunis and Algiers (being North African provinces of the Ottoman Empire) and Morocco had been centers of piracy, preying with a special lust on the ships of the fledgling United States. In March of 1785, Thomas Jefferson and John Adams met in London with the representative of the Dey of Algiers to Britain, Sidi Haji Abdul Rahman Adja. They posed the simple question: Why were the Muslims so hostile to a new country that had done them no injury? Adams joined Jefferson in reporting to Congress through a letter to John Jay, who was then Secretary of Foreign Affairs, that "Islam was founded on the Laws of their Prophet, that it was written in their Koran, that all nations who should not have acknowledged their authority were sinners, that it was their right and duty to make war upon them wherever they could be found, and to make slaves of all they could take as Prisoners, and that every Musselman who should be slain in Battle was sure to go to paradise."

For Jefferson, Islam was a curiosity and beyond the pale of reason, but its anticlericalism and disdain for Christianity had a wry appeal, as it also had for Voltaire, for its destructive influence on the old system of Western beliefs. Considering the vast fortunes being lost to the Barbary pirates and the thousands of Europeans and Americans being captured for slavery, Congress favored appeasement, by bribing the pirates in the form of annual tribute. Adams approved the payoff money, saying, "We ought not to fight them at all, unless we determine to fight them forever." Tripoli broke its truce, and Jefferson launched the Tripolitan War as soon as he became president, though it was not officially declared by Congress. Probably the most significant event at the start of Jefferson's administration was the dispatch of U.S. vessels to the Barbary coast and the march of Army and Marines across the desert from Egypt into Tripolitania, freeing Americans enslaved by the Muslims. There were degrees of enslavement, and not all were repugnant: rather like Joseph in Egypt, it was possible for some to attain rank, like James Leander Cathcart, a United States citizen (having emigrated from Ireland) who worked his way up from keeper of the royal zoo to became a chief clerk to the Dey of Algiers.

Jefferson did not arrange an Iftar dinner for what Obama in his 2010 Iftar address called "the first Muslim ambassador to the United States". Sidi Soliman Mellimelli was not officially an ambassador but a temporary envoy from the Bey of Tunis. Thus "ambassador" was qualified as "envoy" in Obama's 2012 Iftar address, which also added "perhaps" to the claim that Jefferson's dinner for the envoy was an Iftar. Mellimelli spent six months in Washington, fascinating the locals with his charming ways and exotic dress of a scarlet robe, a turban of twenty yards of fabric, and yellow shoes. Indulging the occult, he wrapped Dolly Madison in his cloak, assuring her that it would guarantee the birth of a son. In this he failed. While not formally acceding to Mellimelli's request that concubines be supplied to his hotel, the State Department was able to find a Greek woman named Georgia to keep him company. Secretary of State Madison advised Jefferson that it would be wise to let "pass unnoticed the unique conduct" of this representative of the Barbary states. Mellimelli may have dined at the

Executive Mansion more than once, and customarily at the 3:30 P.M. dinner hour. In Ramadan, he asked to be excused, so Jefferson delayed the dinner for several hours, with no change in menu and without any notion of catering a ritual feast. Cathcart, who had been liberated and returned to the United States, was an escort for Mellimelli and his retinue, because of his acquired Arabic. He noted that the envoy's party did not follow the Islamic rules of temperance and was happy to be acquitted of his charge. Mellimelli's congeniality did not extend to a delegation of Cherokee Indians, whom he called "vile heretics" for following neither Moses nor Jesus. He told Jefferson that he doubted that these Cherokees had descended from Adam.

At the risk of belaboring a trivial point, President Obama was not preoccupied with accuracy in saying that Morocco was the first nation to recognize the United States as a sovereign state. While the city-state of Dubrovnik (then the Republic of Ragusa) claims that honor, and France also has claim through its military agency in the revolutionary period, the Netherlands was actually the first, acting through the Dutch island of Sint Eustatius. While visiting there in 1939, President Roosevelt unveiled a plaque that says: "Here the sovereignty of the United States of America was first formally acknowledged to a national vessel by a foreign official."

While these matters may have been so submerged in arcane history that they fail to appear on presidential teleprompters, it is fair to read John Adam's sense of Islam in what John Quincy Adams distilled:

> The precept of the Koran is, perpetual war against all who deny, that Mahomet is the prophet of God. The vanquished may purchase their lives, by the payment of tribute; the victorious may be appeased by a false and delusive promise of peace; and the faithful follower of the prophet, may submit to the imperious necessities of defeat: but the command to propagate the Moslem creed by the sword is always obligatory, when it can be made effective. The commands of the prophet may be performed alike, by fraud, or by force.

Adams was not only aware that Islam promoted history's largest slave system, including over a million Europeans and tens of millions of Africans, but had even nibbled at New Englanders. In 1625, Governor William Bradford lamented that one of the Massachusetts Bay Colony's ships, in the English Channel within view of Plymouth, had been boarded by Turks who took the captain and crew as slaves to Morocco. The sultan there, Moulay Ismaïl, pride of the Alaouite dynasty, kept 25,000 white slaves. He was known to test his latest axes and knives on slaves, but for that purpose he used Africans.

In his most recent Iftar speech, President Obama said "Indeed, you know that the Koran teaches, 'Be it man or woman, each of you is equal to the other.'" Hundreds of thousands of men, women, and children slaves in Sudan, Chad, Niger, Mali, and Mauritania do not know that. In the nineteenth century, Saint Josephine Bakhita was enslaved by Arab traders in Sudan and forced to convert to Islam. Her saga is a reminder that President Obama's exegesis of the Koran is nuanced. That is especially unfortunate for women and should be a concern to those like Sandra Fluke who spoke at the recent Democrat convention of a Republican "war against women". Sura 47:4 of the Qur'an tells Muslim men: "[Forbidden to you also are] married women, excepting your slave-women." Unlike the Christian scriptures, whose portents are interpreted by the same Church that canonized them, the Qur'an claims to be the very dictation of the Almighty, not one single letter of which can be changed. This then makes Sura 9:123 awkward for citation in an after-dinner speech: "O you who have faith! Fight the faithless who are in your vicinity, and let them find severity in you, and know that Allah is with the God-wary." Happily when Thomas Jefferson hosted his Non-Iftar dinner, he did not quote Sura 47:4 in his Non-Qur'an: "When you meet the faithless in battle, strike their necks. When you have thoroughly decimated them, bind the captives firmly."[1]

During his terms in office, President Obama has betrayed a frail connection with facts by some of the claims he has made, for instance: Renaissance thinkers thought the world was flat, George Washington lived in the White House, Rutherford B. Hayes rejected the telephone, Muslims invented printing, Mexico was independent before the U.S., Austrians speak "Austrian", there are fifty-seven states in the Union, Canada has a president, the death camps were Polish (the Polish Prime Minister called Obama "ignorant and incompetent"), there is no precedent for the Supreme Court overturning a law passed by Congress, his uncle helped liberate Auschwitz (unlikely unless he had been in the

---

[1] Translations of the Qur'an are from the Online Quranic Project: al-quran.info.

Soviet Army), one bomb was dropped on Pearl Harbor, the U.S. government built an "intercontinental railroad". How former presidents should occupy their time in retirement is not indicated by the Constitution, and they are free agents in that regard. They could spend some of their days boning up on history, but it would be better if they had known some history before being elected to become part of it.

9

VACATION TRIALS AND TRIBULATIONS

I T IS NOT MY PRACTICE to take vacations. They strike me as a form of
surrender, like Evacuation Day in New York City, which marked
the end of the British presence in Manhattan on November 25, 1783.
In fact, the last shot of the Revolutionary War was fired that day on
jeering crowds from one of the departing royal ships. It is still com-
memorated annually here by decreasing numbers of people who for
some reason celebrate the cultural suicide of New York. It cannot go
on forever, though, since our schools teach nothing about our past: this
year on Independence Day, most people on Jones Beach were unable
to answer a television reporter's questions about what happened on
July 4 and who was the first president of the United States. But every
vacation strikes me as a form of evacuation with results not quite as
dire as the disappearance in 1783 from our shores of the last ethnic
group with a command of the English language.

I am one with Dr. Johnson, who, when asked if the Giant's-Causeway
was worth seeing, replied: "Worth seeing, yes; but not worth going
to see." Against my better judgment, and at the urging of numerous
people with mixed motives, I took a vacation in July. A retired bishop
had told me I should take one. I objected that I had no need to go
away, since I love what I do and do not need a vacation from it. He
replied that I may not need a vacation, but perhaps my parish does.
So off I went, accepting a kind invitation to the Gulf of Mexico for
three days. My first mistake was to fly, since everyone who knows me

Originally published in *Crisis Magazine*, August 8, 2012.

well knows that there is some inexplicable jinx on me when I take an airplane. If there are a hundred flights scheduled and one is canceled, it will be mine. The last time I defied this curse was earlier this year, to attend a wedding in Australia for one full day and two nights. It is hard for me to get substitutes in my parish, so I rarely spend an overnight away, but going to the other side of the planet for just a day did prove something of a strain, especially as on the way over, there was a power failure, and then a bogus terrorist scare, after which, two hundred miles over the Pacific, a man behind me had a heart attack. The jumbo jet turned around, and we flew to Pearl Harbor under circumstances more benign than in 1941. We were greeted by an ambulance and a group of grass-skirted senior citizens from the Honolulu Chamber of Commerce singing Aloha songs. After waiting almost a whole day, we were bundled back on the airplane. There was a further delay because of a tardy catering service. Everyone agreed that we did not need food, since it was hard to tell by that time what the meal should be. It seemed to be the consensus that all we needed was a capable bartender. Fortunately, the ill man was saved, although most of us felt that we were on a trajectory to the grave. So I arrived in Sydney with only a few hours before the wedding.

Now back to my mandated holiday. During the three days at the Gulf of Mexico, which I could tell, just by looking, was much larger than New York harbor, there were constant tropical storms with fierce lightning, and only one window of opportunity for swimming. As I do not take the sun well and am acronychal by nature, I had little chance to test the waters for sharks. My family has inbred judiciously and injudiciously since the Norman Conquest to attain a sickly pallor, which provokes remarks from hardier outdoorsmen. I did not betray my ancestors. For the rest of those few days, there was nothing to do but watch informally dressed people waiting in long lines to eat a wide assortment of fish in restaurants, most of which had gift shops featuring the same sort of costume jewelry that can be had on lower Lexington Avenue at a discount. The fish were similar to kinds indigenous to the Hudson River except for unattractive creatures with suction cups. I have no appetite for anything that can cling to a ceiling.

My return flight from Pensacola was delayed more than five hours because of a mechanical problem. This required changing my connecting flight twice. Because I had a funeral scheduled for the next day,

I tried to place a telephone call to my parish saying that I might be spending the night in Atlanta, whose modernist airport could benefit from a visit by General Sherman. I do not have a mobile telephone, and when I asked for the location of the nearest telephone booth, it was as if I had requested an astrolabe. There was one "public telephone" requiring an expensive "phone card" with operating instructions that only an engineer from Caltech could understand. Everyone including children now have "cell phones" that are said to damage the brain. I saw evidence of that medical caution all around me. A kindly woman in the airport souvenir shop selling taxidermied heads of small alligators as paperweights lent me her mobile telephone, which I gratefully used even though it was bright pink and decorated with floral stencils. I was able to arrive at LaGuardia around midnight, shortly before closing time.

Upon my return, taking an expensive taxi driven by a Zoroastrian who shared my critical opinions of Al Qaeda, I was moved to kiss the ground of Park Avenue. Then I lost my wallet, which contains everything necessary for survival except oxygen, which so far is still free in our country. It was proper punishment for not traveling with just a walking stick and sandals, which advice indicates that our Lord himself did not think in terms of long trips. At least I made the funeral as scheduled. It has been my long experience that the beloved departed, though dead, always are punctual for their funerals, while brides, though alive, usually are late for their weddings.

G. K. Chesterton said that "travel narrows the mind."[1] By this he meant that we appreciate things foreign when they are far away, but when we travel and encounter them, we focus on how different we are from them. I pray that I may keep my anxious vow, frequently broken, never to fly again. As a theologian, I know that if God had wanted man to fly, he would not have given us the railroad. So that is all I have to say about the strange custom of going on vacations. For my part, I spent the rest of the summer happily in my parish, taking advantage of the general evacuation of the locals, to study German, do some boxing, paint a landscape, and practice my violin—which has the benefit of driving the flocks of pigeons from my roof. Curiously, my own

---

[1] From "What I Saw in America", in vol. 21 of the *Collected Works of G. K. Chesterton* (San Francisco: Ignatius Press, 1990), 37.

neighborhood was filled with vacationers from other places, including a young couple with three children taking a break from the Gulf of Mexico. I am persuaded more than ever before of the wisdom in Noel Coward's song: "Why do the wrong people travel, travel, travel, When the right people stay back home?" A higher authority is Saint Paul, who traveled only of necessity and was beaten, shipwrecked, and stung by scorpions in the process. He said, "When you live in New York, you don't have to travel because you are already there." Or perhaps it was another one of those saints. But it is true.

10

THE QUINTESSENTIAL—
AND LAST—MODERN POET

T S. ELIOT was the quintessential modern poet by being the last modern poet. The ability to speak of the modern in the past tense exposes a nervous tension in the concept of the modern as "the only now", isolated from time past and future. I am aware of no other age that was so self-conscious: the Greeks did not think of themselves as classical, nor did the Scholastics think of themselves as medieval. But modern people justified everything they did by calling it modern. The end of the modern age was not like the end of any other age, for the essence of modernity was that it was not supposed to end: and so while other ages contribute their echoes to the development of culture, the modern age erased itself by succumbing to the future. Like John the Baptist, who was the greatest of the prophets by being the last of them, so was Eliot the most blatant voice of modernism by ending it when he wrote the *Four Quartets*. What comes next is yet to be grasped, but the vague and properly vacuous term "postmodern" means that the only substance of modernity, its unsurpassibility, was a phantom.

The blood and bones of Eliot spanned the modern age. On the day of his birth, the newspapers carried the latest news of Jack the Ripper; and the day he died, Lyndon Johnson proposed his "Great Society". Edison invented the kinetoscope as Eliot was born; and Penzias and Wilson confirmed the "Big Bang" theory with their evidence of

Originally published as the foreword to Thomas Howard, *Dove Descending: A Journey into T. S. Eliot's Four Quartets*, (Sapientia Classics; San Francisco: Ignatius Press, 2006).

cosmic microwave background radiation as Eliot's ashes were being sent to East Coker. It is as if he were finally providing a footnote to his lines by means of his own biology: "What we call the beginning is often the end. And to make an end is to make a beginning. The end is where we start from." The exhaustion of living through modern changes, like any exhaustion, is the ground of depression. Thus the dolors of *The Waste Land*. But if the end is where we start from, there is a cure in the permanent Augustinian metaphysic that is not intimidated by chronology. The *Four Quartets* are a hymn of confidence.

Even in our litigious age, it is difficult to sue universities for philosophical malpractice. Much as I revere the dappled lawns of my New England college days, I have a case against some of my teachers, for they made me wallow through *The Waste Land* with no mention of "Burnt Norton" or "East Coker" or "The Dry Salvages" or "Little Gidding". What they taught about Eliot was equivalent to saying that Saul of Tarsus was a driven man who had roughed up the first Christians, without mentioning his Damascus Road and consequent epistles. The impression was that Eliot had been cut from the same cloth as the chic French existentialists. When my French professor, who idolized Sartre, put his head in a gas oven, it would not have surprised me if Eliot had been next. Instead, Eliot died a natural death just a few months before I graduated. By then I knew that he had a different view of things. It was almost forensically that one read in his obituary in *The Times* how "few . . . saw through the surface innovations and the language of despair to the deep respect for tradition and the keen moral sense which underlay them." Reading those courteous lines now, any tears dry at the enormous condescension of those well-meaning funereal words written in 1965. Having a deep respect for tradition is like saluting an earthquake, and a keen moral sense sounds like the happiness that comes from good dental hygiene.

The *Four Quartets*, like the *Odyssey* and I suppose every poem, really, are meant to be heard. It may be carried to eccentric lengths, like the recordings of Dame Edith Sitwell (who, bless her, went to a length in religion greater than retentive Eliot), but it is a fact: Why write in meters if the meters are not to be sung? I tried once, unsuccessfully, to persuade some rap singers on my Manhattan street corner that they were singing the same rhythms that Homer sent around Iona. (You could stretch this and say something similar about the opening tetrameters in section II of "Burnt Norton".) But I think I was correct. The first time I heard the *Quartets* read publicly was by a favorite actress, Prunella Scales, in the University Church of St. Mary the Virgin in Oxford on the centenary of Eliot's birth. She said that her son's headmaster coached her Greek pronunciation. I was entranced by her, as I had been when she played Miss Mapp and Mrs. Fawlty, but I confess that this seemed the only time her script bored me.

The philosopher Elizabeth Anscombe, who was ever patient with my student mind, insisted that Wittgenstein wanted his philosophical texts read as poetry and disdained classical philosophical syntax. At least in terms of shock value, Eliot was brother to Wittgenstein. I am grateful to Thomas Howard for solving the puzzle of why these vivid quintets are called quartets, when the sections have a dangling fifth part. It has nothing to do with the scheme and everything to do with the voices. There are four instruments. Now, Howard proposes along with others that these are the primeval elements of air, earth, water, fire. It is a good argument, and it cannot be called a critic's conceit, but his graceful analysis whetted my appetite. Eliot's concluding cache in "Little Gidding" from Dame Julian's "Shewings" made me go back to her original lines, as she is ventriloquist for the Almighty God of Grace: "I may make all things well, and I can make all things well, and I shall make all things well, and I will make all things well, and thou shalt see thyself that all manner of things shall be well." Dame Julian wrote that on her sickbed in the Black Death; Eliot wrote that in 1942 during the world's blackest war. These tenses—may . . . can . . . shall . . . will—thawing the frozen "only now" tense of the moderns, parallel the four metaphysical realities: what may be done invokes the possibilities of time; what can be done opens the mind to eternity; what shall be done points to undeniable mortality; and what will be done is the benign calculus of faith. The promise "thou shalt" is the final fifth: the act of the will, which makes man a moral actor in the drama of providence.

If I am obliged to write a foreword, I shall be forward enough to say that I was never drawn to Eliot. He does not thrill like Yeats. I knew some who knew him well and who invariably venerated him, although they were usually of an insecure academic sort that snobbishly dismissed his devoted and long-suffering second wife. While Eliot was to me like the old Dean in the nursery rhyme: "I do not love thee,

Doctor Fell, The reason why—I cannot tell", in a Christian sense I still find much in him to love while not confusing this bond of charity with a chain of affinity. For one thing, there was an aura of pedantry about him, whether in the footnotes of *The Waste Land* or in the language pyrotechnics of *Four Quartets*. The generous soul of Thomas Howard assumes that Eliot was as facile with Attic Greek and High German as he implied. Perhaps he was. Eliot's citations are too precise and buttoned. This does not discredit him. His purpose was valiant. Eliot as poet and Waugh as novelist embarked on much the same Christian adventure, just a generation after Belloc and Chesterton, and Eliot was not the misanthrope that blessed Waugh was. All of them, save Waugh to his credit, shared the same ethereal confusions about economics. Eliot was fascinated with Chesterton and said that he "did more than any man of his time" to "maintain the existence of the [Christian] minority in the modern world". He wrote that eulogy the year he published "Burnt Norton", and, for all its piety, one senses a slight reserve like that of *The Times'* tribute to himself. Eliot was more English than the English, and so I suspect that privately he found Chesterton hearty, which in Eliot's fixed Anglo-Saxon vision would not have been a compliment. And Chesterton was a romantic, certainly in his rotund un-Prufrockian verse, by his own boasting, all bangs and no whimpers. *Four Quartets* and *The Ballad of the White Horse* obliquely hymn the same God, but one suspects that the *Ballad* gave Eliot heartburn. In turn, Chesterton would have found Eliot too precious for his pub crawls and rolling English roads, and he misread Prufrock because of that. Parenthetically, I believe that Robert Frost actually wrote the definitive New England poem, "The Road Not Taken", in Chesterton's Olde England village of Beaconsfield. So the strands weave together and unweave, and, because I am not Penelope, I cannot explain it all, but we are dealing with good hearts trying to make sense of the existence of the human heart in a disheartened world. In *Four Quartets*, Eliot comes to the modernist's lattice window like the lover in the Song of Solomon, furtively chanting a benign proposal of which all this world's lights and shadows are intimations, and in his precise and occasionally affected diction, he witnesses to the Doctors of the Church in this: the intellect is supernaturally perfected by the light of glory.

"The end is where we start from." Professor Howard calculates this to the time matrix of the Holy Mass, where the altar becomes the locus of the Catholic eternal now and confounds the isolated modern illusion of the only now. What is not sacramental is pathological, and the Eucharist is remedy for the social pathology that darkened the promise of Eliot's age. Eliot ends with Dante's rose and Dame Julian's revelation, in a domesticated kind of piety that ungirdles itself to bow before beatitude. Had Eliot lived longer, he might have come to the point where, domestic reserve abandoned and ecclesiastical provincialism thwarted, he would have acknowledged that an earlier poet named Gregory the Great was also the Vicar of Christ. Pope Gregory anathematized those who say that the blessed ones do not see God but only a light coming from him. In the social disintegration and moral trauma attendant upon the fall of modernity, Eliot paraphrased it in coruscating ways and radiant rays of words. A poet has no apostolic authority, and his prophecy is by intuition and sensibility to tradition; but when he is true to the truth, aesthetics burnishes his metaphysics and gives him the mantle of an evangelist.

11

VALOR AND VILLAINY IN WARTIME

A RTHUR CARDINAL HINSLEY, Archbishop of Westminster, was such a strong voice against the Axis that when he died in 1943, King George VI expressed frustration that protocol prevented his attendance at the Requiem. When King George V and Queen Mary had attended the Requiem for the exiled Empress Eugénie at the Benedictine abbey in Farnborough in 1920, a stately remonstrance was sent from the Church of Scotland. On the other hand, royal protocols could loosen canonical strictures, and thus Catholic Eugénie was godmother at the Scottish Presbyterian baptism of Queen Victoria's granddaughter and King Edward VII's niece, Victoria Eugénie of Battenberg who in 1906 became a Catholic before marrying King Alfonso of Spain. Her logic was not complex: "If Uncle Eddie can be head of a Church, why can't the pope?" Queen Victoria, protectress of Anglicanism, had been godmother for the son of Napoleon III and Eugénie, her proxy at the baptism in Notre Dame cathedral being the Queen of Sweden, daughter of the adopted son of Napoleon I, Eugène de Beauharnais.

The Prince Imperial, Eugénie's only child, died in South Africa in 1879 fighting under the British flag in the Battle of Ulundi, stabbed seventeen times by Zulu spears. He was wielding the sword Napoleon I carried at the Battle of Austerlitz. The Zulu Hlabanatunga disemboweled him to prevent his soul from seeking revenge. When the body of Prince Napoleon was brought back to England, Queen Victoria donated his tomb to the Catholic abbey. By an odd quirk, one of Cardinal

Originally published in *Crisis Magazine*, August 19, 2013.

Hinsley's episcopal consecrators had been Merry del Val, son of the secretary of the Spanish legation in London and a close friend of the Empress Eugénie. Hinsley had also been Apostolic Visitor to British Africa, including Zululand. Churchill, innocent of ecclesiology, had so admired the cardinal that during World War II he wanted him to be appointed Archbishop of Canterbury.

Over a couple of years I occasionally wrote for *Crisis* magazine about compelling people, particularly well-known Catholic figures like Cardinal Hinsley, as well as others more obscure, who played their parts in World War II, from 1942 to 1943. Later I expanded this research, and the result has just been published as a book called *Principalities and Powers*. My point all along was that the world's most worldwide war, begun for mixed reasons and fought on many fronts, can only be understood in its essential dynamic as a spiritual combat between forces of great good and palpable evil. It had not only heroes and cowards, but saints and sinners, and as it unfolded, the Church's governing and prophetic and priestly duties were on full display. The French editor of a Protestant newspaper wrote: "The militant Catholics in our country have taken a place which is important and, we do not fear to say, preponderant at the head of the movement of resistance, in which very often they have taken the initiative and of which they remain the inspiration."

I would list a sampling of the things I learned in writing the book. For example, on the Vigil of the Assumption in 1942, the Salesians announced that 120 members of their Order had been executed by the Gestapo in Poland. It was the first anniversary of the death of Father Maximilian Kolbe at Auschwitz, by an injection of carbolic acid. A month later, Father Jan Piwowarczk received a new class of seminarians in Kraków, including Karol Wojtyła. As pope, he would canonize Kolbe and beatify the thirty-one-year-old Salesian Father Jósef Kowalski, who was killed for refusing to trample on a rosary.

The eighty-one-year-old auxiliary bishop of Paris, Emanuel-Anatole-Raphaël Chaptal de Chanteloup, wore a Star of David in protest against the deportation of Jews and soon was buried wearing it. The collaborationist Vichy radio mocked Cardinal Gerlier of Lyons for hiding Jews and resistance fighters: he was "an ex-lawyer who late in life became an Archbishop, thanks more to the omnipotent grace of the House of Rothschild than to the laws of Holy Mother Church". When German officials ordered the Jews of Beauvais to register at the municipal head-quarters, Bishop Félix Roeder claimed a distant Jewish antecedent and was the first to register, processing through the street in full pontifical vestments and preceded by an acolyte carrying the Cross.

In the Pacific Islands, the Japanese killed the Vicar Apostolic of New Guinea and a group of his missionaries. Other Catholic missionaries, including an American, Father Arthur Duhamel, were bayoneted on Guadalcanal. Pope Pius XII's message on the Vatican radio on the Feast of the Transfiguration, broadcast in German, said: "God's ship is destined to reach port safely. She will not sink, for Christ is the helmsman, and the gates of hell, the onslaught of the wildest waves and of the spiritual U-boat action ('Geistige U-boot Arbeit') of godless neo-paganism, will not harm her. . . . For while paganism cannot build up, still less can neopaganism, which lacks even that nobility of mind and true humanity which was found in the old pagans."

In Syria, the Nationalist Socialist Party hailed Hitler as "Abu Ali", and the Young Egypt Party called him "Muhammad Haidar". The Grand Mufti of Jerusalem, Haj Mohammed Effendi Amin el-Husseini, visited Hitler, secured the deportation of five thousand Jewish children to death camps, and obtained a promise from Hitler to liquidate the Jews of Palestine after a Nazi victory. In Belgium, the university of Louvain was purged of its Catholic faculty and Mass was forbidden. The Italian Fascist propagandist Roberto Farinacci blamed Allied bombings in Italy on a conspiracy of Myron Taylor, Winston Churchill, British Catholics, the Church of England, and the Vatican. When Christmas came in 1942, *The New York Times* said that Pope Pius XII "is a lonely voice crying out of the silence of a continent".

Almost at the same time, the Bishop of Berlin, Johann Konrad von Preysing, persuaded that Germany had "fallen into the hand of criminals and fools", wrote in a pastoral letter that the world's present miseries were "the result of human contempt for natural and divine law". His secretary, Father Bernhard Lichtenberg, died en route to Dachau, which had an entire wing meant for priests. Among the inmates was Father Titus Brandsma, a scholar of Nijmegen, who gave his rosary to the Allgemeine SS doctor who administered his poison injection. Two months later, a twenty-seven-year-old priest, Father Alois Andritzki, of Dresden, spoke out against the eugenics policies in the Saxon sanatorium in Pirna. By the end of the war, some sixteen thousand patients, disabled or mentally ill, were killed there as "life unworthy of life". In Dachau, Father Alois asked for Communion, and the guard injected him with acid. By decree of Benedict XVI, he was beatified as a martyr on June 13, 2011, in Dresden cathedral.

Typical of the "greatest generation" who defied all reason save virtue to fight the good fight was the RAF's Flying-Officer Charles Robert Cecil Augustine Allberry, killed in action in the Netherlands at the age of thirty-two. The vice-master of his Cambridge college called him "daring and merry as well as kind" and noted that he had already attained, at the age of twenty-seven, front rank as a Coptic scholar by his edition of a Manichaean psalter. He was received into the Catholic Church a little more than a year before his death. No less dashing was the Crown Prince of Saxony, who relinquished all claims to the royal succession in order to become a Jesuit. This Father Georg was found drowned in Berlin under suspicious circumstances. Brendan Eamon Fergus "Paddy" Finucane died at twenty-one, the youngest Wing-Commander in the history of the RAF, having shot down thirty-two German flyers, twenty-six single-handedly. A friend remembered: "A casual onlooker might be pardoned for thinking him a dare-devil type. . . . I shall like to think of him as I saw him the Sunday before he met his death—kneeling down at Mass, saying his beads with complete simplicity."

One hesitates to single out a few if that neglects the thousands, perhaps millions, who attained virtue on a heroic scale. It is easier to let the villains haunt memory, like the Vichy collaborationist Pierre Laval whose cruelty, while calling himself a Catholic, amazed even many Nazis: "Cardinals and bishops have intervened, but everyone is a master of his own trade. They handle religion. I handle government." It is a sentiment with echoes in the halls of governments in our own time, and it thrived on the cooperation of those who compromised their religious conscience. A priest, Monsignor Jozef Tiso, as puppet president of the Slovak State, paid the Germans to deport sixty thousand Slovak Jews for extermination in Auschwitz, making Slovakia the only country to subsidize such deportations. When he was hanged for war crimes in 1947, he went to the gallows in his clerical clothes. Pro-Ustaše Archbishop Šarić of Sarajevo penned an ode to the Croatian dictator Ante Pavelić. Croatia had the highest rate of genocide in proportion to population of any European country. After the war,

Šarić fled to Spain, while Pavelić was hidden by Jesuits near Naples and eventually settled in Argentina. In Yugoslavia, Bishop Alojzije Mišić of Mostar expressed horror at the massacres of Serbs with the complicity of Herzegovina Franciscans headquartered at Široki Brijeg near Medjugorje. Bishop Mišić described hundreds of women and children and elderly men thrown alive into ravines at Surmanci. Eugène Cardinal Tisserant grimaced: the Franciscans behaved "abominably".

If truisms become truisms because they are true, then we may indulge the adage that human nature never changes. Only the presumptuous are sure that had they been alive in another time, they would have been good rather than bad or indifferent. We can only examine our conduct in the generation given to us, mindful of the apostle whose words seem to have been much on the mind of Pope Francis when he recently consecrated the Vatican City State in our perilous times to Saint Michael the Archangel:

> For we are not contending against flesh and blood, but against the principalities, against the powers, against the world rulers of this present darkness, against the spiritual hosts of wickedness in the heavenly places. (Eph 6:12)

12

HUMPTY DUMPTY'S WEDDING

C ONNECTING WITH PEOPLE you would like to have known is a nice hobby, and I can claim to be just three handshakes from Abraham Lincoln and, remarkably, only five documented handshakes from George Washington, which is rare since as president he preferred to bow. Recently at the opera during an intermission of *Turandot*, I put several grateful people three handshakes from Puccini. Alas, a manager of a sporting goods store near Grand Central Terminal was unmoved when I told him that he was now four handshakes from Felix Mendelssohn. Just two handshakes from the Alice of Wonderland, I spent many hours in the rooms she knew when her father was dean of the college where I studied and where Charles Dodgson wrote the stories for her under his pen name Lewis Carroll. Alice Liddell, later Mrs. Reginald Hargreaves, died in 1934 at the age of eighty-two, two years after she visited New York to receive an honorary degree from Columbia University. It was the centenary of the birth of Carroll, and so the degree was something of an oblique tribute to him, who was also a distinguished mathematician and invented the "Dodgson condensation", which is a method of computing the determinants of square matrices. His book on that subject was never made into a film.

While in New York, Alice met Peter Pan, that is, Peter Llewelyn Davies, on whom J. M. Barrie based his book. Queen Elizabeth II has spoken fondly of Barrie reading his stories to her and her sister when they were the young princesses of the Duke of York. As I figure it,

Originally published in *Crisis Magazine*, January 17, 2013.

the honor of her extended gloved hand a few years ago set me three handshakes from Peter Pan, the same degree of separation, or rather connection, one has through the Alice line. In real life, Alice's was not without disenchantments. Her husband, a well-known cricketer, never recovered from the shock of losing two of their sons in World War I, and, in reduced circumstances, Alice had to sell some of her books. As for Peter Pan, he threw himself under a train in London in 1960.

Lest I seem to be wandering, I should make a point, and it is this: one of Alice's favorite characters in the stories was Humpty Dumpty, whose logic served as something of a political satire through the pen of Dodgson, a logician as well as a mathematician and theologian. He did not invent the name Humpty Dumpty, for that probably was what they called a cannon used in the 1648 siege of Colchester during the English Civil War, and it later became the anthropomorphic egg of nursery rhymes. All the King's horses and all the King's men unable to put the cannon together again after the Roundheads had knocked it off a defense wall were those of Charles I. That sounds likely to me at any rate. But Alice's author made Humpty Dumpty immortal in *Through the Looking Glass.* Humpty Dumpty boasted: " 'When *I* use a word, . . . it means just what I choose it to mean—neither more nor less.' 'The question is,' said Alice, 'whether you *can* make words mean so many different things.' 'The question is,' said Humpty Dumpty, 'which is to be master—that's all.' "

That is the question, and one on which the future of our civilization must hang its hat. When the State tries to establish an imperium over nature itself, it vandalizes all sane instinct and abdicates its duty to promote the tranquility of order by tranquilizing it. The carnage both physical and moral issuing from the disastrous legalization of the destruction of unborn children proves that. Now its dismal postlude sounds in shrill attempts to "redefine" marriage. So far, eleven countries have done it, along with nine of our own states and our nation's capital. In Paris, close to a million public demonstrators have opposed the attempt of France's Socialist president to play Master of the Universe, or at least Master of its Universal Laws. George Orwell said, in a review of Bertrand Russell's book *Power: A New Social Analysis,* "We have now sunk to a depth at which the restatement of the obvious is the first duty of intelligent men." It should be obvious to all except the dense and the willfully ignorant that the next step will be to attack the

Church through civil penalties and fiscal appropriations for refusing to accept the authority of the State to invert the natural order of which the State is only a steward. There was a veiled intimation of this in our national discourse as early as a letter to Madison from Jefferson, whose latitudinarian attitude toward religious bodies still had about it something of the cynicism of the French revolutionaries: "This principle, that the earth belongs to the living and not to the dead, is of very extensive application and consequences. . . . It enters into the resolution of the questions, whether the nation may change the descent of lands holden in tail; whether they may change the appropriation of lands given anciently to the church, to hospitals, colleges, orders of chivalry, and otherwise in perpetuity."

Pope Benedict XVI gave all this priority in his address to the Roman Curia on December 21, 2012, widely ignored by the major American media, which seem jealous of their cohabitation with the present government. He established some sort of precedent by quoting a rabbinical voice not from first-century Galilee, but that of the Chief Rabbi of France, Gilles Bernheim, formerly rabbi of the synagogue de la Victoire in Paris and husband of a psychoanalyst.

> [I]f there is no pre-ordained duality of man and woman in creation, then neither is the family any longer a reality established by creation. Likewise, the child has lost the place he had occupied hitherto and the dignity pertaining to him. [Rabbi] Bernheim shows that now, perforce, from being a subject of right, the child has become an object to which people have a right and which they have a right to obtain. When the freedom to be creative becomes the freedom to create oneself, then necessarily the Maker himself is denied and ultimately man too is stripped of his dignity as a creature of God, as the image of God at the core of his being.

As the State did not invent marriage, neither did the Church. But Christ transformed marriage as he did baptism, building upon its nature by investing it with supernatural graces to represent the indissoluble love of the Bridegroom for his Bride the Church. Thus the Council of Trent condemned polygamy as divinely forbidden since it is contrary to the nuptial meaning of the Church, but the Council's theologians hesitated to denounce multiple marriages explicitly as contrary to natural law, for such marriages at least obliged normal conjugal union. The natural fecundity of the marriage bond is mocked by substituting for it a disorder intrinsically infecund. Our Lord's miracle at a wedding, the first of the seven Johannine miracles, brings to a potency in the spiritual order the seven acts of creation in the physical order. Trying to redefine marriage by human fiat is to pretend that man is creator and not procreator. This old and regressive conceit began with the first lie in Eden: "You will be like God." At the wedding in Cana, Christ's mother said, "Whatever my son says to do, do it." We are free not to do what he says, but we are not free to undo what he did. We are free even to play Humpty Dumpty with nature, only asking which is to be master of words instead of acknowledging the Word as Master. But when the social order has a great fall in consequence, all the politicians will not be able to put it back together again.

13

HANGING CONCENTRATES THE MIND

C APITAL PUNISHMENT does not inspire roaring humor in healthy minds, so wit on the subject tends to be sardonic. Two of the most famous examples, of course, are: "In this country it is wise to kill an admiral from time to time to encourage the others", and "Depend upon it, sir, when a man knows he is to be hanged in a fortnight, it concentrates his mind wonderfully."

The first, "pour encourager les autres", is in *Candide*, where Voltaire alludes to the death by firing squad of Admiral John Byng in 1757 for having let Minorca fall to the French. The second was Samuel Johnson's response to the hanging of an Anglican clergyman and royal chaplain, William Dodd, for a loan scam. Byng's death was the last instance of shooting an officer for incompetence, while Dodd's was the last hanging at Tyburn for forgery. Dodd's unsuccessful appeal for clemency was ghostwritten by Dr. Johnson.

It is not my concern here to take a position on capital punishment, which the Catechism (nos. 2266–67) acknowledges is not an intrinsic evil and is rightly part of the State's authority. This is nuanced by the same Catechism's proposition that cases where it is absolutely necessary today are "rare, if not practically non-existent" (no. 2267). As a highly unusual insertion of a prudential opinion in a catechetical formula, this would seem to be more mercurial in application than the doctrine of the legitimacy of the death penalty. Aversion to the death penalty cannot surpass the bounds of prudential opinion for, as Avery

Originally published in *Crisis Magazine*, February 8, 2013.

Cardinal Dulles has said, "If the pope were to deny that the death penalty could be an exercise of retributive justice, he would be overthrowing the tradition of two millennia of Catholic thought, denying the teaching of several previous popes, and contradicting the teaching of Scripture." What is oddly lacking in the pertinent sections of the Catechism is reference to capital punishment as medicinal as well as punitive. Tradition has understood that the spiritual aspect of the death penalty is to "concentrate the mind" so that the victim dies in a state of grace. Simply put, the less I believe heartily in eternal life, the more disheartened I shall be about entering "a far, far better rest that I go to than I have ever known".

That finale to *A Tale of Two Cities* appeared thirteen years after *Pictures from Italy*, in which Dickens described an execution he watched in Rome during the pontificate of Gregory XVI with its chaotic judicial system: "It was an ugly, filthy, careless, sickening spectacle; meaning nothing but butchery." But Dickens noted the presence of monks accompanied by trumpets holding a crucifix draped in black before the twenty-six-year-old highwayman who had killed a Bavarian countess making a pilgrimage to Rome. The execution was delayed until the murderer's wife was brought to him and he at last received absolution. Back in London three years after writing that account, he witnessed in Southwark the hanging of Frederick and Marie Manning, the last husband and wife jointly to be executed in England. His reaction was similar to that in Rome, save that he thought the crowd of thirty thousand more unruly and there was no mention of a religious tone.

In Rome in 1817, Pius VII reigning, Lord Byron saw three robbers beheaded in the Piazza del Popolo, and he also noted the priests attending those about to die, with banners and prayers in procession. The swift fall of the guillotine was preferable to the "vulgar and ungentlemanly" gallows in England. Although Dr. Joseph Ignace Guillotin had promoted the use of the "Guillotine", first called the "Louison", after its inventor, Antoine Louis, a precursor was in use in Edinburgh in the mid-sixteenth century. Regarded as a humane improvement, it was common in many European countries and was used in the Papal States for 369 executions from 1814 to 1870: a chaotic time in which severe penalties were necessary to maintain some semblance of civil order. Giovanni Battista Bugatti was the official papal executioner from 1796 to 1865, having used an axe before the French introduced the guillotine during their occupation of Rome. Under papal rule, there were three normal sites for executions: the Piazza di Ponte Sant' Angelo, the Piazza del Popolo, and Via dei Cerchi. Shooting was a common form of punishment in the brief Austrian receivership of Rome under the Hapsburg Queen Maria Carolina. Thus we have the firing squad scene in the last act of *Tosca*. While the harshest punishment, hanging and drawing and quartering, is often thought of as peculiar to England, it was more common in the Papal States. The last to be killed that way in England were some Jacobite officers in 1745. The sentence was imposed on several Chartist rioters in 1839, but they were given the option of transportation to Australia, which they accepted. When the pope regained possession of the Papal States in 1814, hanging, drawing, and quartering was imposed eleven times until it ended in 1817. For particularly heinous crimes, crushing the head with a mallet, the "mazzatello", continued until 1870.

The nickname of the papal executioner Bugatti was Mastro Titta, a slang for Master of Justice (Maestro di Giustizia). He wore a red cloak and showed ceremonial deference to his victims. Pope Pius IX let him retire at the age of eighty-five with a considerable pension. This pope, beatified by John Paul II in 2000, was unflinching in stressing the importance of public executions as an "encouragement" to others. On June 12, 1855, a deranged hat maker and political subversive named Antonio De Felici chased the Cardinal Secretary of State with a large fork. Cardinal Antonelli escaped unscathed and appealed to the pope to commute the sentence from beheading to life imprisonment on the grounds of the man's mental imbalance but was refused. Mastro Titta had been retired four years and replaced by his apprentice, Antonio Balducci, when the final executions in Rome took place on November 24, 1868. Giuseppe Monti and Gaetano Tognetti had been convicted of killing twenty-five Zouave soldiers in the Borgo. The executions ceased, not out of any policy of penal reform, but because of the loss of the Papal States. Agatino Bellomo was the last to be executed in the Papal States, in Palestrina, on July 9, 1870. When Blessed Pius IX was asked to grant a stay of execution for those condemned in 1868, the pope firmly replied, "I cannot, and I do not want to." He certainly could have by law, which he embodied as state sovereign with "plenitudo potestatis", but by enigmatically saying that he could not, he probably was declaring this a high matter of conscience in the interest of Augustinian tranquility of order as explained by such as Bellarmine, Liguori, Thomas More, and Suárez. It was the establishment of a constitutional national government for Italy in 1870 that made possible the abolition of capital punishment seven years later and its removal from the Penal Code in 1889.

In our own day, when a papal butler was recently arrested, many were surprised that the Vatican City State even had a jail. The Lateran treaty of 1929 provided for the execution of anyone attempting to assassinate the pope within the Vatican. In 1969 capital punishment was quietly removed from the "fundamental law" of the Vatican, without comment and only in Latin, a fact that did not come to public attention until 1971.

The grandson of Saint Elizabeth Anne Seton, Archbishop Robert Seton, long-lived but less loved, wrote that during the course of a holiday in France as a boy, the ceremonious spectacle of a man being beheaded inspired him greatly to think of the dignity of life. He was especially close to Leo XIII and Saint Pius X, who in 1905 reiterated the Roman Catechism of Saint Pius V with reference to capital punishment: "Far from being guilty of breaking this commandment (to do no murder) such an execution of justice is precisely an act of obedience to it. For the purpose of the law is to protect and foster human life."

The medicinal reason for inflicting punishment goes beyond preventing the criminal from repeating his crime and protecting society to encouraging the guilty to repent and die in a state of grace. The vindictive reasoning also has this interest in mind: for by expiating the disorder caused by the crime, the moral debt of the guilty is lessened. In the early years of the nineteenth century, Saint Vincent Pallotti frequently assisted the condemned to the scaffold, as Saint Catherine had done in Siena. He was edified by the many holy deaths he saw while helping the confraternity of San Giovanni, under the patronage of his friend the English Cardinal Acton. Headquartered in the Church of San Giovanni Decollato (Saint John the Beheaded), their rule was to urge the condemned to a good confession, followed by an exhortation and Holy Communion, followed by the grant of a plenary indulgence. The whole population of Rome was instructed to fast and pray for the intention of the criminal's soul.

All other considerations of the machinery of death aside, this paramount regard for the human soul is quaint only if belief in eternal life is vague. Pope Pius XII was so eager for vindictive penalties that he lent the help of a Jesuit archivist to assist the prosecutors at the Nuremberg trials. He met with the chief United States prosecutor, Robert Jackson, and also told a Swiss reporter: "Not only do we approve of the trial, but we desire that the guilty be punished as quickly as possible." This was not in spite of, but issuing from, his understanding of the dual role of healing and vindication. All this should not be remaindered as historical curiosities, for, as Pope Pius XII said, "the coercive power of legitimate human authority" has its roots in "the sources of revelation and traditional doctrine", and so it must not be said "that these sources only contain ideas which are conditioned by historical circumstances", for they have "a general and abiding validity" (*Acta Apostolica Sedis*, 1955, pp. 81–82).

14

WHY WE NEED LENT

L ENTEN DAYS bring two images immediately to mind, at least to my own idle mind. The first is of the bishops' gathering that first established Lent in 325 during the great ecumenical council in the Turkish town of İsnik—then called Nicaea. Some of the bishops there had been mutilated in the persecutions of the emperors Maximin and Licinius. A dubious record says there were 318 bishops in all, but we do know that their fifth canon ordered a time of fasting and penance lasting forty days, which we now call Lent, presumably because Moses, Elijah, and Christ had fasted forty days. There are bishops maimed like those Nicaean bishops today in China, though our government and many corporations have not advertised them. When one of them, Ignatius Cardinal Kung, was released in 1985 after thirty years in prison, he was surprised to learn that the Church's Friday meat abstinence had been changed. Evidently he did not think this an improvement. While his internment had been a perpetual Lent, he thought the mortifications of his brethren in the West had been sustaining him. In fact, it had been the other way around.

The bishops of Nicaea knew the consequences of mortification, the grief of it when inflicted, and the grace of it when voluntarily assumed. So they extended to forty days what first had been a penitential period of three days before Easter. The season was catechetical as well as penitential, preparing catechumens for baptism and collaterally instructing all the faithful. Over the years, the nature of the Lenten fasts

Originally published in *Crisis Magazine*, March 1, 2001.

and penances varied, and not until the seventh century in the West was Ash Wednesday added so that Lent might last the full forty days if Sundays were exempted. As early as the time of the Council of Nicaea, however, the Church in Jerusalem had kept Lent for eight five-day weeks. The word "Lent" comes from the Old English *lencten*, after the season of spring with its lengthening daylight. Christians, bringing to fulfillment an instinct of most religions, have known that some period of mortification as a "prayer of the senses" serves as a prelude to a spiritual rebirth.

The second image that comes to mind when I think of Lent is that of the Church of Saint George in Velabro along the Roman Forum. Unlike the Church in Jerusalem, whose own altars fasted on the weekdays of Lent by forgoing the liturgy, the Church in Rome celebrated Mass every day of Lent and with special ceremony. At the end of their workday, the faithful would gather around the bishop of Rome and his deacons in procession to a church appointed for the day. The Church of Saint George was the station church for the first day after Ash Wednesday, and since Saint George is the patron of soldiers, the traditional gospel reading for that Thursday was about the centurion who asked Christ to heal his servant. To that church in the course of his tumultuous pontificate during the eleventh century, Pope Urban II brought a portion of the skull of the great martyr George. Others of his relics are entombed outside what is now the entrance to the Ben Gurion Airport in Israel.

When I was living in Rome some years ago, it fell to my lot to preach each year at Saint George on the Lenten station day, beginning when I was a deacon. By then, George's official status on the Church calendar had been reduced in the neuralgic spirit of the late 1960s, though he continues to be the most honored saint—except for Mary—in many Christian nations. Last year, Pope John Paul II undid the revision of the feast, making Saint George's Day a solemnity in such nations as England and India. And of course, like the Nicaean bishops in their endurance, the survivors of Soviet Russia have restored Saint George to their banners, and a new Church of Saint George the Mega-Martyr shines in the sun across Red Square from the sullen tomb of Lenin the Martyrer. Ostpolitik is gone, and Saint George remains.

Lenten Lightweights

All this is by way of saying that Lent is not for the fey. That is because Christianity is not for them, either. Sentimentalists who are Catholics on their own jerry-built terms have no place for Lent. Cafeteria Catholicism, their fast-food version of the heavenly banquet, is neither feast nor fast. Its pastiche of Catholicism has become an anthropological vignette whose day is already past. The felt banners and ceramic butterflies that replaced crucifixes in the late 1960s and 1970s are fading away to the land of kitsch—detritus of the liturgical Martha Stewarts of their day. There is even a rumor that genuine observance of Lent is coming back. The anticipatory "gesima" Sundays that preceded Ash Wednesday before the Second Vatican Council, for all their psychological usefulness, unfortunately may have gone the way of all fleshlessness (pray to Saint George Redivivus for their return), but at least the sense of Lent perdures.

I live in the middle of Manhattan, where Ash Wednesday is perhaps the most popular religious day of the year, albeit confused with Mardi Gras the day before and being quickly surpassed in popularity by Halloween. Thousands come to the Catholic churches for ashes, many without full knowledge of what the ritual really is but at least palpably aware that we are dust. Even the bulimic syntax of the English translation of the rite cannot rob our sense of mortality of a pathetic majesty. We are an Easter people, and, as Saint Augustine was wont to say, Alleluia is our song. But without confession of our many morbid betrayals of the living God, the song becomes a ditty, and instead of the scarred bishops calling the people to repentance as at Nicaea, the Paschal landscape is festooned with harmless adults dressed as rabbits hiding eggs from bewildered children.

Thomas Merton recalled in *The Seven Storey Mountain* that before he became a Catholic, his Easter consisted of an abbreviated service of Morning Prayer followed by an egg hunt on a manicured lawn. Such Easters are like the festivals in the twilight of imperial Rome when, as Suetonius records, the great men spoke of the gods but secretly consulted the stars. Some have so lost confidence in the Resurrection of Christ that they keep little of Lent at all. There are places where there are Ash Wednesday and Easter and in between an extended Saint

Patrick's Day. Great Patrick would be the first to cry out against this from the heights of Croagh Patrick, his fasting place for all forty days.

One could go to the other extreme and think of Easter as merely an interruption of a yearlong Lent. That is the piety of the rigorist for whom every silver lining has a cloud. Worse, there are certain Catholic types with the mottled spiritual complexion of the Jansenist nuns of Port Royal, who were "pure as angels and proud as devils". Patrick lit a Paschal fire, not a Lenten fire. All his fasts were for the feast ahead, and he knew that fasting is not only for the self, since in the Christian community one also fasts for the dead. A parable of the Lenten-Easter economy appears in the chronicles of Nennius the Briton and Tírechán the Gael. They wrote separately of how Patrick fasted another forty days on Mount Aigli near the end of his life:

> And the birds were a trouble to him, and he could not see the face of the heavens, the earth or the sea on account of them; for God told all the saints of Erin, past, present and future, to come to the summit of that mountain which overlooks all others, and is higher than all the mountains of the West to bless the tribes of Erin, so that Patrick might see [by anticipation] the fruit of his labours, for all the choir of the saints of Erin came to visit him there, who was the father of them all.[1]

First, fast to starve the devil, then feast with the saints.

Fasting, Not Dieting

For a long while, when there was a compact and coherent Christendom, Lent as the "truce of God" was a palpable social fact: charity was flaunted, wars were suspended, and executions were postponed. This last was not because anyone thought capital punishment was intrinsically evil. It was because the law courts closed for Lent. To meet the Lenten deadline (yes, I said deadline), executions in the Papal States were speeded up to get them over with by Ash Wednesday. The salutary moral effects of the papal executions often brought about a celebratory spirit inconsistent with Lenten sobriety. With a flair alien to the mor-

---

[1] Quoted in the entry for St. Patrick in Herbert J. Thurston, S.J., and Donald Attwater, eds., *Butler's Lives of the Saints*, 2nd edition (Allen, Tex.: Christian Classics, 1996) 1:615–16.

bidly edifying public posture of contemporary social engineers, the papal executioner sometimes wore a carnival costume. Blessed Pius IX's octogenarian executioner killed five hundred criminals during several papal reigns, including Pius', but Lent was time off for him.

Lent is an occasion of sin, for it is a time when the flesh is made weak. It is the only occasion of sin that one can seek out legitimately. Saint John Chrysostom preached: "God does not impede temptations, first, so that you may be convinced of your strength; secondly, that you may be humble, not proud; thirdly, that the devil, who may doubt whether you have really abandoned him, will be certain of that fact; fourthly, so that you may become as strong as iron, understanding the value of the treasures which have been granted to you."

Self-denial can strengthen the self as no glib kind of self-affirmation can. In California, I saw an advertisement for a preparatory school in which the top student in the senior class said that the school had taught her who she was, to feel good about herself, and to be satisfied with her choices. This Valley Girl vacuousness would have driven Socrates to drink a second nightcap. For those three smug confidences run afoul of the classical triad of erudition: Self-knowledge is delusional without perception of eternal *beauty*; self-contentment eradicates the civilized discontent born of a quest for eternal *truth*; and satisfaction with one's choices is barbaric if one does not choose eternal *good*.

These transcendentals prefigure the temptations of Christ. During his forty days in the wilderness, the prince of lies would have had him turn stones to bread (nature defined materialistically in contradiction of natural aesthetics and supernatural faith); fly (happiness as vainglory in contradiction of natural wisdom and supernatural hope); and exercise power (morality as artifact of the will in contradiction of natural law and supernatural love). Diabolical deceit accepted instead of rejected now plays out its tragic drama in the wilderness of our schools and other social institutions.

Nonetheless, pilgrim voices still chant as guardian angels descant: "Though I walk through the valley of the shadow of death I will fear no evil." This *cantus firmus* of Lent means taking evil seriously enough not to fear it. To neglect evil is to take the self too seriously, which soon makes the self a fearful thing. This is a stubborn canker in spiritual discipline, and it is especially a problem with mortifications such as fasting, which can be self-defeating when done apart from a transcendent love. Fasting and abstinence should be nonchalant, done with panache, for the life of grace is nothing if it is not graceful. "When you fast, anoint your head and wash your face" (Mt 6:17).

We have all had the experience of meeting or knowing people who make a fetish of fasting, even to the length of weighing themselves in the process. With a deluded spirituality, they claim to fast but only diet. The scales of justice are not in the bathroom. Fasting is meant to teach humility: If I cannot do without a few sandwiches, I should speak with reserve about being a soldier of Christ.

Was it not a special favor from God to watch the joint beatification of Pope Pius IX, Abbot Columba Marmion, O.S.B., third abbot of Maredsous Abbey in Belgium, and Pope John XXIII? It was a happy day for goodly fat people like all three and a day of abasement for aesthetical ascetics in "a sentimental passion of a vegetable fashion" who want only gaunt saints on their prayer cards. Enthusiasts who cut down on food principally to improve their tennis game would be less eager to fast if it added weight. In a perversely affluent culture where thinness is an outward sign of wealth, getting fat is not necessarily a way to humility, but it does guarantee humiliation. To paraphrase Chesterton on the angels, the key to heroic virtue may not be in being light but in taking one's self lightly.

Much Communion, Little Confession

The sacramental economy of Lent acquaints earth with heaven without equating them. The forty days are dialectical (earth separated from heaven) in their stress on dying to the old man and denying the passions and analogical (earth in consort with heaven) by their focus on eternity. If you can get through the treacle in John Keble's volume of poetry, *The Christian Year*, you can abide for a while in fine lines like this for Septuagesima Sunday:

> The Moon above, the Church below,
> A wondrous race they run,
> But all their radiance, all their glow,
> Each borrows of its Sun.

I am told that in the Eastern rites there is a custom of singing Alleluias quietly as Lent starts to remind the faithful of what the season of fast is all about: "Lord, let me know my end and the number of my days." The Western rite's Laetare Sunday in the middle of Lent does something of the same, prompting the faithful to keep an "eschatological perspective" or, more felicitously, to "keep an eye on the prize." Lent is a sublime paradox, weaving the pattern of suffering and joy that is the human condition, mortally tragic for the behaviorist and divinely comic for the graceful.

John Paul II is a case in point. Surely the pope's physical infirmities were a mortification for a man of such spiritual authority. He is the only vicar of the one of whom it was said: He saved others, but himself he cannot save. The sight of the pope so constrained by his illnesses makes him an icon of Lent, and·as he gives his blessing *urbi et orbi* with trembling hands, he is an icon of Easter at the end of days many more than forty.

The saints have reiterated this: Unsought mortifications are more difficult than self-prescribed ones. Patience with long lines at the supermarket, rock music on public address systems, and the wrong people running things can be harder spiritual trials than fasts and vigils. If forty days pass with our thinking we have kept a good Lent, we have kept a bad one. That would break the commandment against tempting God. To tempt God is to put his justice to the test by the ridiculous spiritual impertinence that authors of spiritual manuals delicately call "presumption". It is what provoked the biblical imprecations against meretricious rituals and abominable sacrifices.

This is a point that may have eluded a Catholic archbishop in South Africa who, in an earnest effort to make worship more indigenous, recently proposed sacrificing cows for blood libations at Mass. I never expected to have to take up my pen against animal sacrifice, but new occasions teach new duties. The Eucharistic sacrifice is different from all the other sacrifices of all the religions that have ever tried to appease heaven. First, it is all-sufficient, so we need not turn the sacristy into a butcher shop. Second, it is rational and therefore inseparable from moral truth. In Romans 12:1, Saint Paul declares the Eucharist to be an offering of spirit and mind, and Joseph Cardinal Ratzinger has identified intuitions of this in the ancient Dead Sea and Alexandrian Jewish communities. The moral dimension of the "reasonable sacrifice" (*logikē latreia*) of which Lenten anticipation is a prophecy and an icon is the reason we call this sort of presumption a bad thing, like praying to God without having first incarnated that prayer in acts of

charity or like receiving much Communion and confessing little. We
may tempt God—that is the tawdriest privilege of a free will—but
God is not mocked. Not for long. Presumption has its consequences.
Look at the 360 degrees of desolation around us. Look at our parishes.
Lent should mean more of both confession and Communion, spiritual
reading, examination of conscience, benevolent acts, and prayer issuing
in resolution.

Much Ash but Many Miracles

Modern man has had a long Lent. You could say it lasted the entire
twentieth century. Postmodern spiritual fatigue perversely engenders
a kind of compensatory hysteria: eclectic revivals of blood sacrifice
in sub-Saharan lands and liturgical dancing around altars in suburban
America. As a church, we have been mortified: by neglecting the intellectual case against Christ's cultured despisers; by trusting in bu-
reaucracies and utopian movements; by imputing divine inspiration to
private conceits; by slothfulness in the face of infanticide; by compla-
cency about hunger and injustice; by grossly exaggerating the value of
entertainers and professional athletes while neglecting spiritual heroes;
by confusing tradition and nostalgia; by degrading our artistic patrimony; by banality in the pulpits; by scandals and refusing to speak of
them as unspeakable; by the consecration of mediocrity; by voting for
degenerate Caesars when we had the political power to dethrone them;
by contempt for history; by impatience with God's unfathomable patience; by failing to give God thanks for the grace of living in a time
of so many saints and miracles—in short, by softness in hard times.

   In the same twentieth century of so much ash, we have witnessed
many miracles, which perhaps only a later generation will recognize
as such. Lents come and go, and however we may keep them, there is
always Easter at the end. The Lent-Easter cycle has nothing to do with
the change of season from winter to spring, for south of the equator
everything is opposite. It has much to do with the rhythms of the body
asleep and then awake and much to do with the course of history with
its ups and downs.

   I recall a lady who died a few months ago who often rode a bi-
cycle around Rome and unobtrusively attended Mass at our college
chapel years ago. Only when I first visited her for dinner did I find out

that her home was the Palazzo Doria Pamphili, with its one thousand rooms, and that she was the Princess Orietta and part of the long Roman memory. A friend wrote after her death that when traveling with her recently on the Via Quattro Novembre, they went over a pothole, and she said, "That hole has been there since the war." Civic intimacy of such charm is born of a profound acquaintance with and an even more profound love of the place where one lives.

Nevertheless, of Rome it has been said that one knows it well after a year and not at all after a lifetime. This is even more true of the mysteries of salvation. Every lapse into sin should remind us of the first pothole in Eden. Lent is a small familiarity with the inexhaustible drama of redemption in which eternity transfigures mortality: "When I am weak, then I am strong" (2 Cor 12:10). It is a radical break from all other dispensations whose only response to mortality is to ignore it, to flee from it, or to bury it with horrible dirges. We live many Lents during our lives, and we should not make a big burden of them. We should come to know them well and even cherish them, hot cross buns and ashes and all. But when Lent is done, souls attain to the stature of heaven by having measured their own smallness, and they become strong enough to bask in the blaze of glory by sensing their own fragility and turning it into the transparency of grace.

15

TO THE BAR AND THE BENCH

I N JUNE 1961 a stone was found in Caesarea Maritima inscribed for the dedication of a building by the fifth prefect of the Roman province of Judaea. It was the first discovery of a contemporary record of his name in stone. Pontius Pilate. It bears witness, lest anyone should have doubted, that he existed.

Yet his voice still exists, as it always has, on the lips of every cynic who ever lived: "What is truth?" That was his response when Jesus said, "Every one who is of the truth hears my voice" (Jn 18:37). To belong to the truth is to acknowledge the existence of truth and to desire it.

There is a difference between skepticism and cynicism. The skeptic questions the truth, while the cynic questions the existence of truth itself. A skeptic is cautious about being disappointed by a lie. A cynic has been disappointed. There is a saying: If you hug a skeptic, he'll ask if you really mean it; if you hug a cynic, he'll check to see if you took his wallet.

Pontius Pilate and all cynics have been wounded. Their protective reaction is to mock the very possibility of discerning objective truth.

On his way to die, our Lord had told his apostles, "When the Spirit of truth comes, he will guide you into all the truth" (Jn 16:13). The Living Word himself fulfilled these words at the Resurrection when he said: "Receive the Holy Spirit. If you forgive the sins of any, they are forgiven; if you retain the sins of any, they are retained" (Jn 20:23).

Homily preached at the Red Mass for judges and lawyers, New York Guild of Catholic Lawyers, Church of Our Saviour, New York City, October 2, 2011.

In that moment, Christ instituted the sacrament of Reconciliation. Confession is juridical, and authority to absolve is proper to the apostles. A priest can only exercise it, not just by virtue of his priestly orders, but by delegation from a particular bishop, because it involves a particular jurisdiction, just as a civil judge has his own boundaries of authority and all circuits defer to the supreme tribunal.

Receive the Holy Spirit. The Holy Spirit is the bond of love between the Divine Father and the Divine Son, so vital that he is the third Person of this Holy Trinity. This love proceeds from the Father and the Son and is given to the Church. Christ promises that the Holy Spirit will "guide . . . into all the truth". The Holy Spirit is power from on high, but Christ does not say that the Holy Spirit will lead you into all power. He says he will lead you into all truth.

We ask the blessing of the Holy Spirit upon those who administer justice as judges and promote justice as attorneys, because Christ taught the identity of the Holy Spirit with truth. The truth is bigger than any of us. Of this we are reminded when the priest and the judge both put aside their own clothes and put on robes that smother individuality and fashion and, by so doing, link them with a truth older than themselves and a power that is not their own.

The late Elizabethan philosopher Sir Francis Bacon, himself a cynic, said "Knowledge is power." But hard experience has taught that knowledge of the truth is the key to the right use of power—otherwise, there is just raw power, which does not distinguish between right and wrong.

Church law courts often bear the motto: "There is no love without justice", which is an aphorism for the fact that love without justice is not love at all but sentimentality, and justice without love is not justice at all but legalism. Mix sentimentality with legalism, and you have a diabolical recipe for cruelty. In the twentieth century, totalitarian systems separated power from truth. Once power is autonomous, independent of truth, it is unjust by its self-justification. In those ten decades of the twentieth century, apart from the horrendous deaths in wars, State-sponsored terror destroyed an estimated 170 million lives. Hitler's National Socialism created an anachronistic paganism, while Mao, Lenin, Stalin, and Pol Pot imposed philosophical materialism. In each instance, power was a totality that cynically overwhelmed religion, morality, and law. The sign that Pontius Pilate placed over the head of Jesus on the Cross proclaiming him King was written in the

Hebrew of religion, the Greek of morality, and the Latin of law. As the classical cynics mocked the truth, this may explain why Pontius Pilate said, "Quod scripsi scripsi, What I have written I have written." But even Pilate unwillingly may have been inspired by a higher Spirit when he said that.

As religion for its own sake is superstition, and morality for its own sake is narcissism, so law for its own sake is the cynicism of Pilate: "What is truth?"

One year ago [September 17, 2010], Pope Benedict XVI spoke before the assembled leaders of Britain in Westminster Hall. It was an unforgettable sight, most especially when he stopped for a moment on the spot where Saint Thomas More stood at his trial. Then the pope spoke words which will last as long as anything said in our generation. He said,

> The fundamental questions at stake in Thomas More's trial continue to present themselves in ever-changing terms as new social conditions emerge. Each generation, as it seeks to advance the common good, must ask anew: what are the requirements that governments may reasonably impose upon citizens, and how far do they extend? By appeal to what authority can moral dilemmas be resolved? These questions take us directly to the ethical foundations of civil discourse. If the moral principles underpinning the democratic process are themselves determined by nothing more solid than social consensus, then the fragility of the process becomes all too evident—herein lies the real challenge for democracy.

In Communist Poland in 1953, Cardinal Wyszyński began three years imprisonment, as some two thousand bishops and priests were arrested, theological faculties and parish schools were closed, punitive taxes were imposed on the Church, and the government publicized and even fabricated immorality among the priests and people to demoralize the Church's confidence in herself. Cardinal Wyszyński's crime was to have said from the heart of his tortured country: "We teach that it is proper to render unto Caesar the things that are Caesar's and to God that which is God's. But when Caesar sits himself on the altar, we respond curtly: He may not."

In every age and in every culture, Caesar has a chronic itch to sit on the altar. As there is no love without justice, Caesar has to be taught metaphysical manners. So in our own corner of the world and in our own moment of history, the bishops of the United States have established a special committee for religious liberty. The foundational documents of our nation ensured religious liberty, but the Founding Fathers were not the Apostolic Fathers. George Washington was granted to our nation by a singular providence, and in his wisdom he knew that what the Founding Fathers had ensured could only be maintained by vigilance. In his Farewell Address in 1796, he asked: "Where is the security for property, for reputation, for life, if the sense of religious obligation desert the oaths which are the instruments of investigation in courts of justice? And let us with caution indulge the supposition that morality can be maintained without religion." That Father of our country may have been more utilitarian than any of the Fathers of the Church in his assessment of the economy of divine law and natural law and positive law, but his warning was clear.

Right now, in these mild autumnal days, the Supreme Court is hearing cold challenges to the Free Exercise and Establishment Clauses of our nation's Constitution. At the same time, the bishops of the United States have given six specific reasons why religious liberty is threatened now. The Department of Health and Human Services is seeking to force private healthcare providers to carry contraceptive and sterilization services. That same department wants to force the Church's Migration and Refugee Services to provide what it calls "the full range of reproductive services". The federal government is seeking to impose this on international relief programs. The Department of Justice is attacking the Defense of Marriage Act, arguing that support for the natural law of marriage is a criminal form of bigotry. The Justice Department is attacking a religious liberty known as the ministerial exemption, which insulates religious employers from State encroachment. And the State of New York has defined same-sex relationships as legal marriage with a very narrow and fragile religious exemption.

When laws are legislated that invent as "rights" conduct contrary to natural law, power usurps truth. So Saint Thomas Aquinas said (*ST* I-II, q. 95, a. 2): "Every law made by man can be called a law insofar as it derives from the natural law. But if it is somehow opposed to the natural law, then it is not really a law but rather a corruption of the law."

On December 8, 1942, in France, his primatial see of Lyon colonized by the Nazis, Cardinal Gerlier said from his cathedral pulpit, "The world of the future will be Christian, or it will be hell."

We are in that future, and a verdict has not yet been made about tomorrow. Priests and lawyers may be sobered by the Parable of the Good Samaritan, for it was a bad priest and a bad lawyer who ignored a man who stood for all of broken humanity. The Holy Spirit who leads into all truth has also given us a living parable about two men who spoke truth to power. One was a good priest, Saint John Fisher, whose last public words on the scaffold were, "Send the king good counsel." The other was a good lawyer, Saint Thomas More, who said, "I die the King's good servant, but God's first."

16

SPEAKING WELL OF THE DEAD

O N JULY 29, 1997, a representative *philosophe* of our abortion culture, retired Supreme Court Justice William Brennan, was lav-
ishly eulogized in Saint Matthew's Cathedral in Washington, D.C.,
where the Requiem Mass for President Kennedy had been sung in
1963. Richard Cardinal Cushing was relatively constrained back then,
because liturgical depredations had not yet switched into high gear. It
was not thus when our president, who vetoed the ban on partial-birth
abortions, was permitted to announce to all corners of the cathedral
for consumption in all corners of the world: "Brennan's America is
America at its best." That is, internecine America is at its best with
thirty-nine million fewer children than would have been born were it
not for Brennan's eisegesis of the Constitution. Attorney General Janet
Reno later said in a speech to the American Bar Association that the
honors paid to Brennan in Saint Matthew's Cathedral inspired her to
go on.

As Dr. Johnson conceded, in lapidary inscriptions no man is upon
oath. To avoid testing this protocol in the sanctuary, where only truth
is to be spoken, eulogies were discouraged in more honest days, when
even romanticized charlatans and avuncular Caligulas could be buried,
but with the crepe of contrition. Since Americans became persuaded
that God is a Butterfly, funerals have started to resemble Jeanette Mac-
Donald's airy obsequies at Forest Lawn Cemetery in 1965, with canaries warbling fantasias in gilded cages. Nature had revenge when the

Originally published in *Crisis Magazine*, November 1, 1997.

canaries were released and dropped dead on the heads of mourners, victims of hot air and manifest incontinence. No such favor was granted on July 29 in Saint Matthew's Cathedral when a priest asked from the pulpit: "How does a young man, son of immigrants, rise to such a position of judicial preeminence, with almost the entire government present to honor him on the day of his burial?" It would have been poignant if Saint Thomas More had dropped from heaven right then. A brief glimpse of the saint's head would have been a sufficient reply.

Once in a press conference in which he distanced himself from the angels on significant points of behavior, Senator Edward Kennedy said that Saint Thomas More had been "intolerant". The saint indeed had been intolerant, but of falseness. The logician in him would have found grotesque the Orwellian doublethink of the priest-eulogist who said that one way to honor Brennan's memory would be to help "a young pregnant girl". The jurist in him would have raised an eyebrow when the priest declared: "The Brennan mind met the Brennan heart, and in their perfect match was the secret greatness of our friend." A meeting of mind and heart is anatomically difficult when there is a spine; and when More insisted on this point, his King obliged with an ax. In the majority opinion on *Roe v. Wade*, Brennan concurring, mind and heart congealed to produce the words: "If the human race is to survive, pregnancy will always be with us." The twentieth century has taught that such banality can be the diction of cruelty incarnadine.

Senator Kennedy often seems innocent of historical information, as he was in an interview with an Italian reporter in 1982 when he placed the Battle of Lepanto in the Second World War. This has made him a much sought-after eulogist. Except for his recidivistic neglect of verbs, the rhetorical senator can excel Bossuet on the death of the Prince de Conde. At a requiem for Mr. Stephen Smith, he pictured his father and brothers playing golf on a cloud with his spontaneously beatified brother-in-law. The press quoted this recreational account of the Beatific Vision with murmurs of approval.

It is not that Senator Kennedy should have said anything tactless over the corpse or that he should have mentioned some more vigorous sport instead; he simply should not have been saying anything at all from the pulpit. If Horace Walpole thought Dante was a "Methodist parson in Bedlam", anyone who believes in the Four Last Things might take Senator Kennedy in the pulpit for a therapist in Camelot. The misguided may excuse this because "funerals are really for the family", but that is not so: consolation of the bereaved is a derivative benefit of the first purpose of the funeral rites, which is the offering of prayer and Eucharistic sacrifice for the dead. When that purpose is not understood, the rites themselves may succumb to parallel intuitions of stoicism and sentimentalism. Mix the two into an incongruous brew, and the reaction is nervous banter around the coffin and self-conscious whimsy.

Senator Kennedy is not to be blamed more than some clergymen who blow kisses to reality from a distance. Recently, when a prominent athlete died after a raucous life, a prelate from a cathedral pulpit described Christ the Umpire calling "Safe!" as the man slid into home plate. The anodyne metaphysic was not what Saint Paul meant by running the race. Gone, long gone, is the quality of unction that moved a holy friar in Paris centuries ago to preach exquisitely over a one man slum of a bishop who had died in a lady's arms: "Perhaps Monseigneur's only mistakes were his manner of living and his manner of dying." Any public figure who is the subject of the prayers of such a friar must have a happier frame of mind on the other side of the grave than one whose presumption is frivolously vested as grace.

The Church's rubrics require that anything edifying in the deceased's life be mentioned only as commentary on the Gospel. Our "Culture of Death", as the pope calls it, is idiosyncratic in its refusal to be cogent about the Gospel mystery of death itself. In its rejection of moral reality, this lurid cultural paradigm mocks the imperatives of the mystery by applauding the guilty as cold-bloodedly as it destroys the innocent. Where the idol worshipped by a culture is one's public image, even candor must be sacrificed to it; and when only the self is celebrated, celebrity canonizes itself. All the Holy Sonnets are replaced by one unholy bravado: "Death be proud."

The noble pagans flattered and flowered their dead because they could not absolve them. *De mortuis nihil nisi bonum dicendum est* is not a Christian dictum; speaking nothing but good of the dead translates the Spartan decency of Chilon, who lived six centuries before the Incarnation of the Redeemer. Chilon was a wise magistrate himself and as merciful as a Spartan could be, but his mercy was not that of Christ the Judge, for Chilon had no power to summon the dead: "Come forth!" The noble pagan tried to make the best of a bad thing, urging a social convention born of pessimism. The mercy of God changes pessimism to hope, and hope is the engine of honesty. In obedience to the Divine Mercy, speaking well of the dead may sometimes require not speaking good of the dead. However many different ways there are to say it, everyone has the same eulogy: "One there is who is good. If you would enter life, keep the commandments."

For some, those words are a bit too terse. In a more florid tribute to Brennan, but snobbishly for a populist, Father Robert Drinan of the Georgetown University Law Center wrote: "When we think of Irish Catholics in public life we usually call to mind mayors, local officials and, yes, ward bosses. Brennan shattered all those images. He was an intellectual, a visionary, a prophet. . . . His memory will be forever held in benediction." Although Drinan made no allusion to Mount Sinai, he did compare Brennan favorably with the author of the Code of Hammurabi.

Even in our coarse times, a remnant etiquette should prevail in moments of emotional strain. A veil is drawn over those who grieve, and if Edward Kennedy and Robert Drinan can support each other in mourning the death of William Brennan, they should be allowed to do so. But when they publish their grief, they invite remark. They may even conjure commentary from gaunt ghosts long dead who can tutor lesser cynics in calculation. For all his odd little ways with God, preternaturally cynical Napoleon held trimmers of the Gospel in contempt even as he made use of them. In his memoirs, Chateaubriand describes Talleyrand, ex-bishop of Autun, arm in arm with Joseph Fouché, who had been educated by the Oratorian and was an agent of the Terror, as "Vice on the arm of crime". From time to time, there actually appear on the public scene individuals who can fit that description by hugging themselves.

Descent to the phosphorescent obsequiousness of Mr. Justice Brennan's funeral was greased by the efficient compact John F. Kennedy made in his run for the presidency, telling the Protestant clergymen in Houston that he would never be under the thumb of a pope. He should have stuck to the advice of Pius VII on the lengths of accommodation: "We are prepared to go to the gates of hell, but no further." After Kennedy nudged public Catholicism from the snows of Canossa to the sands of Palm Beach, eulogists claimed that his gnostic kind of religiosity was Catholicism come of age, but it was Catholicism ashamed of its age: God's good servant, but the King's first.

In Camelot this was hailed as prudence, though it was little more than cunning. Saint Thomas Aquinas knew it as *astutia*: morally neutral in its original meaning, but vicious as an excuse for imprudence. It exploited a tribalism that was willing to wink at the roguish ways of any one of the boys who moved on up from the ranks of mayors and ward bosses to become accepted by the chattering classes as "an intellectual, a visionary, a prophet".

One of its kitchiest icons was a painting commissioned by Monsignor Aloysius Dineen of New York, showing Pope John XXIII and President Kennedy together feeding doves. The painting has been removed from the church where it first hung, but it still prompts to panegyrics those who think that Kennedy made it possible for a Catholic to become president, when he only made it possible for a Catholic who behaves like a modern Episcopalian to become president. One positive item salvaged by John Kennedy from his Anglo-Saxon formation was a line repeated every year by the headmaster of the Choate School, the Rev. George St. John: "Ask not what your school can do for you, ask what you can do for your school." He perhaps absorbed the words until he felt free to modify them, as he also did with the Ten Commandments. His extended family may now be in the process of doing the same even to the Code of Hammurabi.

Before there was a White House, Jesus Christ spoke of whited sepulchers. I do not know if this would fall under the category of what Congressman Joseph Kennedy allegedly refers to as "Catholic gobbledygook", but Christ did say it, and he said it because he disdained hypocrisy. According to our friend Dr. Johnson, who was more intuitively Catholic than many putative Catholics: "No man is a hypocrite in his pleasures." If churchmen insist on eulogizing, they might get right to the point by describing what *sort* of pleasures occupied the dead in their lifetimes. The thought could restrain them from jumping into celebrity graves. It certainly would temper any propensity for Shakespeare's "Sweet words, low-crooked curtsies, and base spaniel fawning".

Surreal Catholicism has spawned a neurotic parade of celebrities who think incense is a form of aromatherapy and a harrowing pantheon of politicians who consult *L'Osservatore Romano* less than *George* magazine. What panegyrics will be gassed over them within the House of God? We have cause for concern, given the precedent of the Maeterlinck "there is no death" sort of poetry read over the body of Mrs. Jacqueline Onassis by her housemate.

In the moral order, one may not pass final judgment on another.

Savanarola called that to the attention of a bishop who was damning him to all eternity. One is also required to make temporal judgments according to one's state in life. That is why there are judges. That is why there are social institutions, beginning with the family. That, above all, is why there is a Church endowed with supernal keys and censures. Madness consists in the inability to make right judgments, and it is the very definition of depravity beyond madness to fail to perceive the need for right judgments at all. Our present problem is not the arrogance of damning souls to hell. The plague is of courtiers who subpoena charity to defend sloth and, having so dazzled the jury, proceed to judge publicly that their little lords are in heaven.

The Brennan funeral followed one in Miami for Mr. Gianni Versace, the rich Italian tailor whose work, according to a breathless release from the Catholic News Service, was "noted for its sensual lines and eye-catching combinations of texture and shade". His priest-eulogist baroquely envisioned the murdered man decorating the wings of angels and recalled a promise that if he became pope he would have Versace design the cardinals' robes. Well then, the eulogy might have ornamented sacred rhetoric by adapting Bertrand Russell's assessment of Anthony Eden: "Not a gentleman; he dresses too well." Instead, the preacher burst into song: some lines from a popular Broadway show tune, a toe-tapper to be sure, but not quite up to the *Dies Irae*. Then the neurasthenia went international: another requiem for Versace in the cathedral of Milan featured Elton John and Sting tearfully crooning on the spot where Ambrosian chant was invented.

Later that summer, as Byrd and Handel and Elgar rolled in their graves and the Great Organ of Westminster Abbey was hushed, Mr. John, now raised to the rank of universal banshee, wailed on a piano for the Princess of Wales, who was "the real Queen", according to television reporters who could not tell a Plantagenet from an eggplant. Using as theme music Mr. John's song originally written for Marilyn Monroe, solemn newscasters morphed Diana with Mother Teresa, whom CNN sidelined as "another notable and good woman". It was like the time Ulysses S. Grant told the second Duke of Wellington that he understood his father had also been a military man. Great Wellington, as a man upon oath all his life, would have been a singular eulogist. When a London mob, demonstrating adoration for George IV's hapless and estranged Caroline of Brunswick, threatened not to let him pass until he cheered her, the Iron Duke answered from his high horse: "Well, gentlemen, since you will have it so—'God save her!'—and may all your wives be like her."

There may be those who agree with the above but confide that it would be better all around if it were not said. In the second volume of the *Historical Sketches*, introducing Chrysostom, John Henry Newman cautiously refers to "the endemic perennial fidget which possesses us about giving scandal; facts are omitted in great histories, or glosses are put upon memorable acts, because they are thought not edifying, whereas of all scandals such omissions, such glosses, are the greatest."

How odd it is that a society that has made a fashion of apologizing for every *auto da fé* in Spain and every slave auction in Savannah will not apologize for sycophancy and cynicism. Many, apparently, do not have time to go to confession because they are too busy begging public forgiveness for the slaughter of Hypatia. Gratuitous apologizing for the crimes of other ages and people is dangerous humbug, said C. S. Lewis; it weighs in well with the press, but less so on the scales of justice, for it can be detraction masked as contrition. At the same time, Never Never Land finds indecipherable what C. S. Lewis meant by authentic penance and accountability.

If eulogies are not sensibly stopped, I do hope they will be more precise than what was said at Justice Brennan's cathedral rites: "Wisdom tells us that the souls of the just are in the hands of God." I am all for wisdom. So much so that I question whether we are to assume that a man is just by having been declared a Justice by his government. I am so much for wisdom that I fear the souls of the unjust might be in the fists of God. I am even so much for wisdom that I hope a merciful God will not squeeze his fists too tightly. And I am so completely for wisdom that I remember how the finger of God once wrote a eulogy on the wall of Belshazzar's feast. From the perspective of those who thought Belshazzar charming, the graffiti was in bad taste. But the party was over, and the sweet singing canaries were dead on the floor.

17

REMEMBERING THE JESUS SEMINAR

THREE MAJOR NEWS MAGAZINES did it this past Easter season. One should feel guilty about letting these journals set the agenda for theological discourse, or for any discourse, for that matter. C. S. Lewis thought that the reading of any magazine was bad for one's English. It cannot be better for one's theology. But what is not said says it all: The face of Jesus on the cover of a secular magazine sells more copies than the image of anyone else who has ever lived.

On April 8, 1996, *Time* featured a split image of the Holy Face. Thirty years before, to the day, it ran the pictureless cover: "Is God Dead?" As a student in New York back then, I was fascinated by the way a glossy magazine could send such a chill down the vestigial spines of so many theologians. The fact that Christ appears on the cover now, albeit drawn by some Eutychian in *Time*'s art department, may underlie the anxiety of those who gamble for the seamless garment of the man whose words they largely dismiss.

They would have to believe that something so unscientific as casting lots in a California resort hotel two thousand years after the event is more reliable than listening to the voices of those who had first been part of the event, like the one who made a concluding point: "This is the disciple who is bearing witness to these things, and who has written these things; and we know that his testimony is true." A spokesman for the Jesus Seminar, who rejects the entire Fourth Gospel but says his own testimony is true, claims that he left the priesthood and took

Originally published in *Crisis Magazine*, February 3, 2012.

a wife as the result of inconsistencies in the Synoptics. By a similar reasoning, any Shakespeare scholar should drop all his incongruent folios
and take a whole harem.

Nothing is new about remarking the lack of science in pseudoscience
about the Scriptures. The Catholic modernists Loisy and Tyrrell, blind
to their own flaws, saw the cracks in German historical criticism in
the nineteenth century. Martin Kähler had seen the same earlier when
he distinguished between the historical Jesus and the historic (that is,
suprahistorical) Christ. But that was just another variation of the Kantian mood that, along with Hegelianism and Romanticism, became the
mental ether of the age. At least Kähler challenged the inculturated presumption of subjective historical critics. In a winter term lecture at the
University of Berlin in 1899, the erudite Adolf Harnack would boast:
"The Germans mark a stage in the history of the Universal Church.
No similar statement can be made of the Slavs."

At the time, a ten-year-old boy in Austria, already hoping for an artistic career, knew nothing of this; but he would find useful resources in
those advanced cultural notions when he became führer of the Third Re-
ich. In 1909, even Albert Schweitzer could write: "Nowhere save in the
German temperament can there be found in the same perfection the living complex of conditions and factors—of philosophical thought, critical acumen, historical insight, and religious feeling—without which
no deep theology is possible."

Spurious Scholarship

We are not superior for seeing through the sentimental unwinding
of the nineteenth century that gave us the Teutonic Christ. We may
be more culpable at the end of the twentieth century for replacing
that stolid modernity with a capricious postmodernity and coming up
with a Californian Christ who sounds like a hybrid of Ralph Nader
and Maya Angelou. Whimsy builds upon whimsy, and we are told with
half-concealed pathos that Judas was not a betrayer and that this "Jesus-
Lite" had several siblings noticed in the past only by a few Nestorians.
This passes as scholarship in the Flamingo Resort Hotel in Santa Rosa.

The panelists there took seriously the apocryphal Gospel of Thomas,
while ignoring recent paleographical evidence for dating some canonical texts earlier than the year 70 (including Matthean material, if the

Magdalen College papyrus fragments are substantive). Dr. John A.T. Robinson, whose name was almost synonymous with the "Death of God" controversy, even argued in his last years for a radically earlier date for the Johannine texts. But he is dead, and officially dead people do not attend the Jesus Seminar.

Thoughtful Latin stoics and Semitic Sadducees would not have considered the Jesus discovered in the Flamingo Resort Hotel worth killing. It is sobering, however, to consider that the president of the United States said that he prayed deeply before vetoing the ban on partial-birth abortions. Perhaps the Jesus of the Jesus Seminar is the sort of Messiah who hears such prayers from the White House and replies in mellow tones, "OK."

This brings to mind that nun who a few years ago said of a genially beclouded prelate: "He affirmed me in my OK-ness." The pervasive inarticulateness of our times surely has roots in the philosophical autism of which that poor woman was a lurid example. The problem has become too widespread to be noticed by many. It has conditioned a quest for the historical Jesus that is less like a Victorian expedition to a dark continent and more like a sensitivity session. This is not to say that the historical Jesus is elusive. He is the measure of historical meaning. The Incarnation is the template of all births and deaths. The historical Jesus is not the problem; the subjectivity of the quest is. Schweitzer noticed that his own teachers had tended to fabricate the Lord in accordance with their own character. That is nostalgic reverie posing as history. Nostalgia is history after a martini.

Sometimes liturgical revisionists cast their own lots as languidly as any dilettante in a Jesus Seminar by purging from the lectionary references to Satan, the order between husbands and wives, the Fatherhood of God, and the hard sayings about fire and flesh. Or some may take on the cheerful task of suburbanizing the whole Gospel, like the "Contemporary English Version" of the American Bible Society that greets the entry of Jesus on Palm Sunday with the refrain, "Hooray for God in heaven above!"

Logic of Logos

God seeks man and finds him hiding behind a tree. In the Upper Room, he comes to men who are huddled in confusion, and from the shore he calls to men pulling empty nets—scenic icons of his appeal to post-modern man on the edge of a nameless age. When a novice asked how to find God, a mature monk answered, "Open your eyes." Two figures in dazzling apparel asked the women at the tomb, "Why do you seek the living among the dead?" At the Ascension, two similarly dressed figures asked, "Men of Galilee, why do you stand looking into heaven?" It is hard at the end of this millennium to admit that these figures have pure intelligence, for we had hoped that by this time we might have it. But we can listen to those who do have it, and they say that Christ is not an artifact. He comes into history as history and is discerned by locating the self of his events. "But seek first his kingdom and his righteousness, and all these things shall be yours as well."

Precisely in obedience to this logic of the Logos, Saint Augustine, in his commentary on Genesis, warned against using Scripture as a prooftext for natural phenomena. Aquinas was of the same mind (in *De Caelo et mundo*, bk. 2, lesson 17). And so, too, in the encyclical *Divino Afflante Spiritu*, Pius XII distinguished the levels of interpretation according to literary genres: discursive, allegorical, analogical, and so forth. All of which may seem esoteric if one dismisses more texts out of hand. Textual criticism is semantic embroidery outside the communal grace of ecclesial life, for talk about the historical Jesus is chatter unless it starts with talk to Jesus at our moment in history, which is prayer. The Church's teaching on scriptural inspiration is part of this divine commerce, a teaching that is most importantly expressed in the Church's prayer, the liturgy.

In *Mystici Corporis*, Pius XII condemned the proposition of contradictions between the external juridical elements and internal mystical elements in the life of the Church. In 1907, Tyrrell had indeed posited that dichotomy. He used as an example the spirituality of Saint Bernard of Clairvaux, whose combination of scholasticism and mysticism was to the modernist like oil and water. A certain will-o'-the-wisp renewal in contemporary Church life has proceeded on this analysis, animated by the "transcendental Thomists" who effectively manipulated liturgics and catechesis, in an internal *Kulturkampf* more destructive than any external assault in the annals of Christianity.

I suspect that men are being ordained to the priesthood today who have never read a single sentence of the Second Council of Orange. If they had, they might be more aware that the critical issues that seem novel have had a long past and have been addressed by better minds. Both Vatican Councils alluded to this economy, and so did the seminal encyclicals on exegesis: Leo XIII's *Providentissimus Deus* of 1893 and Pius XII's *Humani Generis* of 1950. They witnessed to this crucial rubric: the appearance of contradictions in inspired texts is evidence of contradictions in our cognitive faculties, and the right use of reason requires that higher criticism acknowledge this.

The Brief Record of Jesus

The brevity of historical records about Jesus is a natural argument for their authenticity. This includes extracanonical witnesses, like Polycarp's testimony from John recorded by Irenaeus. Legends would be more detailed because the gods of legends are invented: much of the best pagan literature is poetic detail about the gods. This is also the case with early Christian apocryphal texts; and it is precisely because of the Church's historical sense that she has relegated these to the class of apocrypha. In contrast, the appearance of Christ, and many of his sayings, are taken for granted in the canonical texts and not mentioned, precisely because he is granted to the human intelligence and not invented by it. *The Book of the Acts of the Apostles* is a major, and in many ways unique, advance in classical historical narrative. Its attention to facts should humble the social historians and psycho-biographers of our generation. But it is familiar with Jesus the way ideologues are not.

So its record of his worth and the apostolic response to them is biographical chiefly as a biography of the Church. It does not conjure up a historic Christ in suprahistorical counterpoint to any historical Jesus. The Church rejoins from experience: "Remember your leaders, those who spoke to you the word of God; consider the outcome of their life, and imitate their faith. Jesus Christ is the same yesterday and today and for ever." He who is and will be is none other than he who was.

The evangelists are conscious that their own lives are determined by this mystery, so they do not write their "own" gospels. There really is no warrant for speaking of "Matthew's Gospel" or "Luke's Gospel" as you might speak of "Euclid's theorem" or "More's *Utopia*". There is one Gospel, that of Jesus, written "according" to them. *The Book of the Acts* is an astonished reflection of Christians on how "the outcome of their life" is not a federation of lives, but the singular life of Christ alive in them as the Church. This kind of astonishment is a switch from the bewilderment of those who had walked with Jesus toward Jerusalem, becoming faint of heart. Subjective criticism apart from the Paschal mysteries will always be relegated to that mental state.

On those who stay with him along the road, the Lord confers an authenticity that they did not have. This is Christ's search for the historical man. Man is historical in Adam; he becomes historic in Christ. Those who died in Adam become alive in Christ by drinking of Christ's cup and being baptized with his baptism. Once the Word is made flesh, the flesh of the Word is more than words. He is the articulation of personality. Saul becomes Paul on the Damascus Road when he realizes that in the lives he is persecuting is the life of Christ. For Christ does not speak of "them" but of "me" when he speaks of the Church.

In this new realism follow pastoral letters, not syllogisms. And the baptized speak of this reality to palpable people straining to be more real themselves. When Paul speaks without trembling before Gallio, he speaks before the brother of Seneca, who, as a Cynic, lived only as half a man by philosophy. But even half a man, if he cannot shed light, can cast a shadow. Not one of these characters is a mere symbol. Recently, when lecturing outside Rome along the Appian Way, all my rambling words were the weakest commentary on that to which historic Peter and Paul had reconciled themselves as they walked on those historical stones.

How Confusion Travels

Here is the sacred tradition at work and not nostalgia, eschatology, and not ideology. The Gospel, after all, issues in a Book of Acts and not a Book of Ideas. Ideas, however, can usurp acts when the ego mimes reality. Not unlike biblical critics of his day, Nietzsche crowed about a "sixth sense", which was the "historical sense" developed by the human race only in the nineteenth century. He went mad; but there are those who, after the wreckage of a whole moral slum of a century, still invoke his sixth sense in Jesus Seminars and the like. All this would be delicate academic nonsense were it not for a couple of world wars and the lakes of blood flooded by the post-Kantian fantasy that denied reality. It is our age of revisionist history, and not the apostolic age, that should be on trial. Of all the lines Jesus spoke, which dull minds and heavier hearts would rather think he had not spoken, there is none more awful than the question that sounds in decibels louder than ever: "Have I been with you so long, and yet you do not know me?"

On another recent trip, I saw tourists riding past the chateaux of the Loire on their way to see the plaster castle of that cultural Chernobyl: Euro Disney. There Eleanor of Aquitaine abdicates in favor of Cinderella. And as I said Mass in the cathedral of Rheims, I had the impression that there were some visitors there for whom Joan of Arc was Ingrid Bergman and who, if they saw Margaret Mary Alacoque and Catherine Labouré in their glass coffins, could not have told them from Sleeping Beauty. The capacity of older cultures for memorization and accurate oral tradition has evaporated.

From our new low vantage point, it is assumed that Christians, and especially Christian saints, have twisted history, even when Christianity gave culture the elements of historical science and the essential reason for wanting to know history, just as it gave the impetus for the inductive methods of physical science. And this we are told by a collapsing culture; 90 percent of those latest bachelors of arts have read no classical history and have no language other than an idiomatic corruption of their own. Yet Bernadette Soubirous was so simple and straightforward that she asked her Lady to write down her name and handed her a pen to do it; a modern Jesus Seminar has too much guile to be that graphic.

The plain Christian veneration for sacred sites, pilgrimages, and relics testifies to its information about places and things. Some still mock this, but a residual sense of place and character perdures. Those who might wink at the archeology of Helena or Etheria make a business of tourism, if not to the City of David, then to the City of Disney. The Pearl of Great Price may be neglected, but there are those who pay six-figure sums at Sotheby's for a celebrity's fake pearls.

Words False and True

In this moment we suffer from a logjam of words about the Word. When hope is alive, heart will speak to heart, as Saint Francis de Sales prayed it might. That is how the Sacred Heart must surely have spoken to the Immaculate Heart, in some of the most certain unwritten words of Jesus. Some critics may have lost heart for the words of Jesus because of the way Christians speak his words. Translators may understandably be vexed in trying to combine accuracy with vitality, but in the effort, opportunities can be lost.

For example, the profundity of the encyclical *Evangelium Vitae*, like so many grand documents, was done a disservice by the translation into English, which describes the Garden of Eden as a place of "harmonious interpersonal relationships". In 1994, priests around the world received the *Directory on the Ministry and Life of Priests*, whose unfortunate syntax told the toiling shepherds: "Pastoral charity constitutes the internal and dynamic principle capable of uniting the multiple and diverse pastoral activities of the priest and, given the socio-cultural and religious context in which he lives, is an indispensable instrument for drawing men to a life in Grace." If the historical Jesus had spoken that way on the Galilean shore, I doubt that Peter would ever have left the sociocultural and religious context in which he lived and made it to the sociocultural and religious context of Rome.

It is not strange, then, that the sheep are scattered on a thousand hills and that there is some question whether Jesus really did speak of heavenly things. If man would speak of love in lovely arabesques, he must will to love. "He who does not love me does not keep my words; and the word which you hear is not mine but the Father's who sent me." It cannot be clearer than that in this world, unless what passes for clarity is the agreeable myopia of some historical critics. Someone remarked when told that David Hume was clear: "All shallows are clear." Those are the shallows in which people at unlovely Jesus Seminars paddle.

All history is the Emmaus Road. Two men two thousand years ago were conducting their own Jesus Seminar on it, until Jesus himself took over. "What is this conversation which you are holding with each other as you walk?" The next millennium will be shaped by the answer this age gives him. We have less excuse than those first pedestrians for giving a pedestrian reply. God is merciful, but the mercy is twin to justice.

As Arius was judged by an ethereal assize the day before he intended to force sanction for his contempt of the Word, the twentieth century should expect no less. If reparation is not made, there will come upon churches as well as nations a darkness and sorrow such as the world has not known. In that bleakness, which is already a culture of death, no Californian Christ will appear, but only the terrible beauty of the Most Holy and Undivided Trinity.

18

THE CASE OF MRS. JESUS

MONSIGNOR RONALD KNOX, probably the most inspired preacher and apologist of the twentieth century, wrote an essay in 1928 satirizing some skeptical biblical literary critics, in which he used their methods to "prove" that the real author of Tennyson's *In Memoriam* was Queen Victoria.

Many who doubt the plausibility of the Scriptures are gullible about hoaxes. I do not just mean the rabbit with antelope horns called a jackalope. There was the Cardiff Giant of 1869 promoted by P. T. Barnum, and John Payne Collier's forgery of Shakespeare letters. Some pretended to be the Grand Duchess Anastasia, and far earlier was the hoax of a lady pontiff named Pope Joan. The New York Zoo hoax of 1874 convinced many that animals had escaped. Henry Ford promoted the "Protocols of the Elders of Zion". While it is not certain that Teilhard de Chardin was one of the perpetrators of the Piltdown Man ruse in 1912, Stephen Jay Gould was convinced that he was a principal player in fabricating the so-called Eoanthropus. There were aliens landing in Roswell, New Mexico in 1947, and the Balloon Boy hoax in 2009. The *Da Vinci Code* claimed an albino monk hid corpses nearby on Thirty-Fourth Street. I confess that I keep a warm spot in my heart for the Loch Ness Monster, which also intrigued Pope Pius XII, who discussed it with the above-mentioned Ronald Knox. Unfortunately, Nessie's primary witness was an English vicar, and such testimony is not potent in courts of law. And let us not forget the

Originally published in *Crisis Magazine*, October 2, 2012.

many pious but parochial Catholics headed for the hills with packaged rations during the Y2K scare at the start of the Third Millennium.

Hoaxes gain credibility when they use respected sources. In 1938, Orson Welles' adaptation of H. G. Wells' *War of the Worlds* convinced thousands because it was broadcast on radio. Monsignor Knox did something similar on the sacrosanct BBC in 1926 with his amusing "Broadcasting the Barricades", which reported the toppling of Big Ben, by trench mortars and the torching of the Savoy Hotel and the lynching of a cabinet minister. That may actually have stirred up the devil in Welles. People today are inclined to believe hoaxes because they are mentioned witlessly in the mainstream media.

In 2002 *The New York Times* spent a lot of printer's ink on a bogus ossuary reputed to be that of a "brother" of Christ. The *Times* as well as the *Washington Post* featured this on their front pages with measured solicitude, although neither journal gives such publicity to huge events such as the annual pro-life gathering in the nation's capital. Recently the same journal announced on its front page the discovery of a fourth century parchment translating a second century Greek text, claiming that there was a Mrs. Jesus. Shortly thereafter, the parchment was judged a forgery by Coptic experts. If a correction ever appears, it will be in fine print back in the shipping news section. Or at least on page 8, which is where, in the same week, *The New York Times* reluctantly reported Pope Benedict's Mass for 350,000 in Lebanon—an event that astonished nearly everyone except our mainstream media.

As *The New York Times* generally gives the impression that anyone who takes the Scriptures seriously is archaic and arcane, there is an inconsistency in that newspaper's affectation of interest in the Christology dormant in Abysinnian paleography. Since journalists often invoke pretentious scholarship to challenge the authenticity of the Shroud of Turin and the Tilma of Guadalupe, one is forced to ask: Why do these people suddenly become so credulous about phenomena that contradict Christian inspiration? The answer speaks for itself. *The New York Times* would be delighted to find that Christ did not radically contradict the norms of his age by forsaking all else and calling others to do the same as a proclamation of the Mystical Union between Christ as Bridegroom and the Church as Bride: " 'Let us rejoice and exult and give him the glory, for the marriage of the Lamb has come, and his Bride has made herself ready; it was granted her to be clothed with fine linen, bright and pure'—for the fine linen is the righteous deeds of the saints. And the angel said to me, 'Write this: Blessed are those who are invited to the marriage supper of the Lamb.' And he said to me, 'These are true words of God'" (Rev 19:7–9). But these are not the words of *The New York Times*, whose editors do not include the Good News among "all the news that's fit to print" and whose inverted anthropology prefers to give frequent and gushing coverage in its "Styles" section to ceremonies uniting bridegrooms with bridegrooms and brides with brides.

Those branches of the media which of late have become flamboyant propagandists of State policies, should, but obviously do not, take the counsel of Saint Paul, who probably would be fired after his first day at work as an editor of *The New York Times*: "As we have said before, so now I say again: If any one is preaching to you a gospel contrary to that which you received, let him be accursed" (Gal 1:9).

19

THE EUTHANASIA EUPHEMISM

DURING A DEBATE on the Senate floor in 1996, at the time of President Clinton's veto of a bill to ban partial-birth abortion, there was an incident reported in an article in the *Washington Post*:

> Not five feet away, Republican Senator Rick Santorum turned to face the opposition and in a high, pleading voice cried out, "Where do we draw the line? Some people have likened this procedure to an appendectomy. That's not an appendix," he shouted, pointing to a drawing of a fetus. "That is not a blob of tissue. It is a baby. It's a baby." And then, impossibly, in an already hushed gallery, in one of those moments when the floor of the Senate looks like a stage set, with its rich wooden desks somehow too small for the matters at hand, the cry of a baby pierced the room, echoing across the chamber from an outside hallway. No one mentioned the cry, but for a few seconds no one spoke at all.

On February 13, 2014, when the Belgian Chamber of Deputies approved by a vote of eighty-six to forty-four an amendment to its 2002 euthanasia law, extending its provisions to include the killing of children, a man in the gallery cried out, "Murderers!" Again, no one mentioned the cry, but there was an awkward silence until the man himself was silenced for exhibiting bad taste. He had dared to remove the linguistic fig leaf from the euphemism "euthanasia". A euphemism covers shame, a timid confession by syntax rather than by sacrament, for a euphemism wants approval and not absolution.

Originally published in *Crisis Magazine*, February 19, 2014. (King Philippe would sign the euthanasia bill into law on Sunday, March 2, 2014.)

Others have cried out, including a faculty member of Leuven University, Tom Mortier, whose mother had been "euthanized" in April 2012 without his permission by Doctor Wim Distelmans because she was chronically depressed. Since then, legislators decided that children should share with adults a supposed right to be euthanized, when their present life is judged by the State, parents, and the children themselves to be "unworthy of life". This resonates with the well known language of two university men, the jurist Karl Binding and the psychiatrist Alfred Hoche, whose 1920 treatise *Die Freigabe der Vernichtung lebensunwertes Lebens* gave an academic veneer to the consequent and more impatient Nazi protocols for "destroying life unworthy of living". Soon enough, vehicles rounded up the unfit, adults and children, with covered windows and sealed doors so that those inside could not be seen or heard. In 1941, a teenaged cousin of Pope Benedict XVI, with Down Syndrome, was taken away in that fashion by "therapists" despite his family's pleas and never to be seen again.

The twentieth century was littered with failed utopias called workers' paradises and other thousand-year reichs, the imaginings of men with fertile minds, while unspoken was what fertilized them. Saint Thomas More invented the term "Utopia" for his exercise in irony, a description of heaven on earth, possibly in some place of which he had vaguely heard, now known as Brazil. In it he describes its use of euthanasia by ingestion of laudanum. Some have assumed that this, and other Utopian innovations, such as docility to miscreants and marriage of priests and even occasional women priests, were recommendations of the same More who sentenced heretics to death. A college textbook used in New York and evidently written by someone innocent of Greek actually describes him as an early champion of euthanasia. But his Utopia is seen through the eyes of Raphael Hythlodaeus, whose name means "dispenser of nonsense" and might also be translated Binding or Hoche. More's unspoken point is that this Utopia is Platonism carried to such an extreme that it does not connect with reality. After all, Utopia means "No Place", quite as another place More mentions, "Macarensis", is "Happyland". And he knew that bliss born of ignorance is stillborn. More would have understood that other sort of Christian, Milton: "The mind is its own place and in itself can make a Heaven of Hell, a Hell of Heaven."

The kingdom of heaven is real and not a Utopia, and that is why the

Christian can be neither a utopian nor a cynic. At the Versailles Conference, seated between Wilson and Clemenceau, David Lloyd George thought he was seated between Jesus Christ and Napoleon. But Jesus Christ was not a utopian, and Clemenceau was misunderstood as a cynic. He was shrewder than that, and shrewd enough to invoke God, with whom he had a tenuous relationship, saying of Wilson's Fourteen Points: "Even the good Lord contented himself with only ten commandments, and we should not try to improve upon them." The abandonment of sense for sentimentality leads to dangerous territory, and we should always be cautious when we see political leaders receiving flowers from beribboned little girls and saying that all they do is "for the children". In *The Thanatos Syndrome*, Walker Percy put it with unyielding, if gratifying, honesty (echoing Flannery O'Connor): tenderness leads to the gas chambers.

By high irony, what was "Bleeding Belgium" at the end of World War I has voted to bleed itself to death with an admixture of extravagant utopianism and cynicism. King Albert II, father of the new king, Philippe, hoped that his son would be "an inspiration for Europe" as he was fit for the job "emotionally and intellectually", having been at the Belgian Royal Military Academy, Oxford, and Stanford. Philippe's saintly uncle, King Baudouin, abdicated for one day in 1990 rather than sign into law a bill permitting abortion. The King of the Belgians now has only moral influence, but moral influence outlasts political influence, even if victims of power do not. If Baudouin's nephew confounds expectations and refuses to give the Royal Assent, he will honor his uncle, who asked parliament, "Does freedom of conscience apply to everyone except the King?" Should he yield, his figurehead role will be so disfigured that his picture will serve a purpose only on the other side of the postage stamps.

The United Nations, if too cynical to persist in its foundational utopianism but cynical enough to accuse the Catholic Church of encouraging child abuse, will now have to square the Belgian Law with its own 1959 Declaration of the Rights of the Child and its 1966 International Covenant on Civil and Political Rights. But that organization, perhaps esteemed more by the Holy See over the years than it has respected itself, is likely to continue to accommodate its own declarations to the exigencies of our culture of death. After all, among the members of United Nations Committee on the Rights of the Child are [in 2014]

Thailand, which hosts an active child sex slave trade, Uganda, whose army enlists children, and Syria, which kills children with poison gas.

This is not only Belgium's problem. Immediately after February 13, a regular columnist in the *Los Angeles Times* wrote that "for a child facing death in the short term, and in agony, we as a society should enable the child's right to die with the least amount of suffering. . . . Even if the concept chills us to the bones." That was only a short remove from 1991, when the *New York Times* bestseller list featured a book by the Hemlock Society on how to commit suicide. A chain of bookstores in New York listed it in its section on "Self-Improvement". In 2003, the Hemlock Society changed its name to "Compassion and Choices".

There is a macabre risibility about the Belgian provision that says that when parents and physicians decide to kill, "the child must be conscious" of their decision and demonstrate a "capacity of discernment". Our own Supreme Court held in *Roper v. Simmons* (2005) that the Eighth Amendment forbids the execution of offenders who were under the age of eighteen when their crimes were committed, since the capacity for full moral judgment is still formative in adolescence. Certainly it cannot be less so in childhood.

In 1943, Blessed Alois Andritzki, a twenty-eight-year-old priest of Dresden, was given a lethal injection in Dachau. His efficient crime was to have decried the "merciful death" (*Gnadentod*) program ("Action T-4") begun in 1939 by Hitler's attending physician Karl Brandt. Father Andritzki's church had been nearby the euthanasia center at the Saxon sanitorium in Pirna. An acrobatic gymnast, Andritzki would perform stunts to cheer up fellow inmates slated for almost certain death. Perhaps in an upside-down moral culture, one must do that to keep balance. One thing is known, if unmentioned in parliaments and senates, and it is plain: When the cry of a baby is heard from a gallery, it comes from far beyond that, for it is from the Cross. "But we impart a secret and hidden wisdom of God, which God decreed before the ages for our glorification. None of the rulers of this age understood this; for if they had, they would not have crucified the Lord of glory" (1 Cor 2:7–8).

20

LAUGHING WITH CAESAR:
RELIGIOUS FREEDOM

O F THE 427 WEDDINGS in my present parish during the past eleven years (I have lost count of all the others), the band—for want of a better word—at the most recent reception was the loudest I can remember. Conversation was impossible, so some of a certain age complained loudly but not loudly enough, and others of a lesser age laughed at their complaints. I have come to realize that for many of them, conversation as an art is an unknown thing.

This reminded me of the line about the morally tranquilizing effects of "intolerable music" in Solzhenitsyn's 1978 Harvard Class Day address. On another Class Day four years later, Blessed Teresa of Calcutta mentioned Jesus thirteen times, but the edited account of her speech in the *Harvard Magazine* gave no indication that she had mentioned him at all. The 1978 speech upset far more commentators than the offended scholarettes in Cambridge who stomped their feet at Mother Teresa's mention of virginity and the protection of unborn babies. Rosalyn Carter responded at the National Press Club in a speech reported to have been written by herself: "Alexander Solzhenitsyn says he can feel the pressure of evil across our land. Well, I do not sense that pressure of evil at all." She added that Solzhenitsyn would not have accused America of shallow materialism if he had known about our many voluntary organizations that bring neighbors together. Evidently, news of those wonderful groups such as the United Way had never reached the

Originally published in *Crisis Magazine*, November 20, 2012.

121

Gulag to cheer the inmates. But what really made the lovers of intolerable music hiss Solzhenitsyn in 1978 was his warning: "On the way from the Renaissance to our days we have enriched our experience, but we have lost the concept of a Supreme Complete Entity which used to restrain our passions and our irresponsibility. We have placed too much hope in political and social reforms, only to find out that we were being deprived of our most precious possession: our spiritual life."

As he spoke, *Pravda*, the newspaper named for truth, was still a megaphone for the lies of Moscow. It censored his speech. Things have changed. These days, the *Pravda* of the Russian Federation is quoting Solzhenitsyn. In an article (July 1, 2012), Xavier Lerma cited his 1978 address and went on to say that Obama is president because of America's "immorality and materialism". Then the *Pravda* writer quoted John Adams: "Our Constitution was made only for a moral and religious people. It is wholly inadequate to the government of any other." The litany went on: "Abortions financed through tax dollars now total fifty million babies killed. Their blood cries out to Heaven while Hollywood justifies abortion and some women call it a choice. . . . The other half of America stands against this evil tide with constant prayer while their public protests are not completely shown by the American media." The writer invoked the contempt Lenin had for the beclouded liberals of the West sympathetic to him, whom he called "useful idiots", and compared them to the present generation of obtuse Americans: "these 'useful idiots' will still blame Bush for the economy, overlook Obama as they overlooked Clinton's mistakes. . . . The communists won while Americans smoked pot."

In 2008, *L'Osservatore Romano* hailed Obama's election as "a choice that unites". Westerners got Obama wrong, as they also got others wrong. At Mussolini's rise to power, the Dean of the College of Cardinals, Vincenzo Cardinal Vanutelli, said that the Duce "had been chosen to save the nation and restore her fortune". Churchill early on had called Mussolini a "Roman genius . . . the greatest lawgiver among men", and Roosevelt referred to him, perhaps with a timbre of Hyde Park condescension, as "that admirable Italian gentleman". But when Pope Pius XI learned the facts, he flung burning indignation at the Fascists.

That is the lesson: It is possible for those accustomed to the insulation of rank to come to their senses. It is even possible to find a Becket or two among them. But in the French Revolution it was easier for the Abbé Grégoire to set up a Constitutional Church docile to the new social order, while the faithful clergy went to the scaffold or became galley slaves in Guyana. To avoid turning into some sort of neutered National Patriotic Church, Catholics must witness to the government that human rights are of natural law and are not doled out by the State to citizens who obsequiously request them. Passive resistance to the suppression of religious liberty is obedience to the law of natural order. This will test the mettle of the faithful. As the Apostolic Nuncio to the United States, Archbishop Carlo Maria Viganò, said in an address at the University of Notre Dame: "Martyrdom may not necessitate torture and death; however, the objective of those who desire to harm the faith may choose the path of ridiculing the believers so that they become outcasts from mainstream society and are marginalized from meaningful participation in public life."

If the Church is to be prophetic in our toxic culture, truth must trump dilettantish ideology. That means freeing the Church from the deadweight of a self-perpetuating bureaucracy myopic to threats on the horizon. Benedict XVI said: "The bureaucracy is spent and tired. . . . It is sad that there are what you might call professional Catholics who make a living on their Catholicism, but in whom the spring of faith flows only faintly, in a few scattered drops."[1]

Consider how the archbishop who chaired the draft committee for the 1986 pastoral letter of what was then the National Conference of Catholic Bishops, "Economic Justice for All", considered Reagan morally derelict. The letter's flaws were addressed by laymen who knew about economics, such as William Simon, J. Peter Grace, and Michael Novak. The document was mercifully put to sleep by John Paul II's encyclical *Centesimus Annus*. In 1983 the NCCB had also opposed Reagan's foreign policy in another pastoral letter, "The Challenge of Peace", whose prescriptions would have helped to fortify the Berlin Wall. A prominent Irish bishop was sympathetic to it and refused to shake Reagan's hand during the president's state visit to Ireland. Subsequently, that bishop was obliged to leave his country for South America, the archbishop responsible for the letter on economics

---

[1] Benedict XVI, *Light of the World: The Pope, the Church, and the Signs of the Times: A Conversation with Peter Seewald*, trans. Michael J. Miller and Adrian J. Walker (San Francisco: Ignatius Press, 2010), 59, 141.

retired in unhappy circumstances from his archdiocese, which eventually filed for bankruptcy protection, and the silver anniversaries of those tarnished pastoral letters have passed in silence.

When free people vote against their own freedoms, they pull down the columns of a free society on themselves, the way Samson brought down the temple on his own head. The first column to collapse would be the First Amendment right to freedom of religion. Naifs who thought this could not happen will be startled when the Church has to close charities, hospitals, schools, and even parish churches if they are subject to tax intimidation. In the long run, this would be far more disastrous to our civilization than looming fiscal chaos and international belligerence provoked by foreign perception of our domestic lassitude.

Since so many voters rejected sound warnings, at least a beacon of honesty now shines on the Catholic Church in the United States. The seventy million or so Catholics were a Potemkin Village, and the number of faithfully practicing Catholics are a small portion of that number. On November 6, the Protestant vote went for Romney over Obama 57 percent to 42 percent, while the Catholic vote went for Obama over Romney 50 percent to 48 percent, Those who hoped that immigrants would bolster the Church must consider the 71 percent of Latinos who voted for Obama, an increase of 4 percent since 2008. Actually, everyone has suffered from the neglect of catechesis in the past forty years. Catholic universities and religious orders were allowed to become engines of dissent. In one of our nation's most respected seminaries, after a debate before the last election on the role of conscience in voting, only nineteen out of fifty-two of our future priests supported Romney. Long before he became pope, Benedict prophesied, "[The Church] will become small and will have to start afresh more or less from the beginning."[2] As Leviathan's lions begin to roar, the nominal Catholics will skip out of the arena. Roman Catholicism has become for baptized pagans a neuralgic kind of Cute Catholicism, with leprechauns, mariachi bands, and Santa Claus instead of confession, prayer, and fidelity to doctrine. But behind each leprechaun Saint Patrick stares, and behind every mariachi band Our Lady of Guadalupe weeps, and behind every Santa Claus Christ himself judges.

---

[2] Joseph Cardinal Ratzinger (Pope Benedict XVI) *Faith and the Future* (San Francisco: Ignatius Press, 2009), 116.

Catholics could have saved the best in America and they can only blame themselves and their promotion of an entitlement culture for the collapse of the temple and its moral distress: redefinition of marriage, family breakdown, politically correct speech, contempt for chastity, a record low birth rate, and destruction of infants. As William Butler Yeats wrote in "The Second Coming", quite likely in reaction to the Russian Revolution of 1917:

> Things fall apart; the centre cannot hold;
> Mere anarchy is loosed upon the world,
> The blood-dimmed tide is loosed, and everywhere
> The ceremony of innocence is drowned;
> The best lack all conviction, while the worst
> Are full of passionate intensity.

We are not a Christian nation now. In 1783, Washington spoke of "our blessed Religion", and on D-Day Roosevelt prayed for "our nation, our religion, and our civilization". This would not be allowed in our secularized culture. Shepherds of the faithful cannot charm into reason the forces that now preside over our nation. We can dance to Caesar's intolerable music, but he will call the tune. We can feast with Caesar, but he will soon feast on us. We can laugh with Caesar, but he will soon laugh at us. *Risus abundat in ore stultorum.* There is abundant laughter in the mouth of the foolish.

21

GOVERNOR PLINY AND GOVERNOR CUOMO

G AIUS PLINIUS CAECILIUS SECUNDUS was governor of Bithynia-Pontus in present day Turkey from A.D. 111 to 113. That capped a long career during which he served as judge, staff officer, knight, senator, quaestor, tribune, praetor, prefect, consul, propraetor, and augur. He was popularly known as Pliny the Younger because his uncle, the naturalist and military commander, adopted him. When the Elder died, probably of asphyxiation, at Stabiae, during a rescue attempt when Vesuvius erupted over Pompeii, young Pliny was saving his mother at Misenum. Given his acrobatic balance in dancing to the tune of very different emperors: Vespasian, Titus, Domitian Nerva, and Trajan, he reminds one of Talleyrand, whom he actually surpassed in erudition as a writer of Greek verse and orator in the line of Cicero. Talleyrand would have admired his cynicism, as when he decried Domitian as soon as he died, having long extolled him. It is curious, but not atypical of the Italian Renaissance, that this torturer of Christians should be honored with a statue on the façade of the cathedral in his native town of Como.

A growing body of Christians was unsettling the pagan establishment in Bithynia. Pliny wrote Trajan a famous epistle beginning with the flattery he had mastered:

> It is my constant method to apply myself to you for the resolution of all my doubts; for who can better govern my dilatory way of proceeding or instruct my ignorance? I have never been present at the

Originally published in *Crisis Magazine*, January 27, 2014.

examination of the Christians [by others], on which account I am
unacquainted with what uses to be inquired into, and what, and how
far they used to be punished; nor are my doubts small, whether there
be not a distinction to be made between the ages [of the accused]
and whether tender youth ought to have the same punishment with
strong men? Whether there be not room for pardon upon repentance?
or whether it may not be an advantage to one that had been a Christian, that he has forsaken Christianity? Whether the bare name, without any crimes besides, or the crimes adhering to that name, to be
punished? In the meantime, I have taken this course about those who
have been brought before me as Christians. I asked them whether they
were Christians or not? If they confessed that they were Christians,
I asked them again, and a third time, intermixing threatenings with
the questions. If they persevered in their confession, I ordered them
to be executed; for I did not doubt but, let their confession be of any
sort whatsoever, this positiveness and inflexible obstinacy deserved to
be punished. There have been some of this mad sect whom I took
notice of in particular as Roman citizens, that they might be sent to
that city.

Pliny deemed these people superstitious because "they were accustomed to meet on a fixed day before dawn and sing responsively a
hymn to Christ as to a god." Superstition was not a crime, and it was
rife in the empire, but these Christians refused to worship the gods
of the land and would rather die than worship the Emperor himself.
There were not a few Christians who got cold feet and obliged Pliny:

A libel was sent to me, though without an author, containing many
names [of persons accused]. These denied that they were Christians
now, or ever had been. They called upon the gods, and supplicated to
your image, which I caused to be brought to me for that purpose, with
frankincense and wine; they also cursed Christ; none of which things,
as it is said, can any of those that are really Christians be compelled to
do; so I thought fit to let them go. Others of them that were named
in the libel, said they were Christians, but presently denied it again;
that indeed they had been Christians, but had ceased to be so, some
three years, some many more; and one there was that said he had not
been so these twenty years. All these worshipped your image, and the
images of our gods: these also cursed Christ.

Trajan wrote back saying that Pliny had followed proper procedure,
but to be fair according to Roman justice, the "spirit of our age" re-

quired that the governor should only persecute those who refused to cease being Christians.

Governor Andrew Cuomo recently declared on a radio program in Albany that those who uphold, by implication, Christian moral standards and refuse to go along with state legislation on such matters as abortion and the redefinition of marriage have "no place in the state of New York". If this also applies to dead New Yorkers, perhaps he should exhume the remains of pro-life feminists like Susan B. Anthony and Elizabeth Cady Stanton. He did not threaten to throw anyone to wild beasts, but the tone of the governor of the Empire State was decidedly imperious, and the threat of having to move west of New Jersey might be unsettling to even the most devout Catholic New Yorkers. As Cuomo has publicly flaunted his concubinage with the cook Sandra Lee, it cannot be said that he is inconsistent in his moral prescriptions. If hypocrisy is the tribute that vice pays to virtue, he is the very opposite of a hypocrite, for he would rather insist that virtue pay tribute to vice. It is unlikely that a statue of Governor Cuomo will ever adorn the Albany cathedral like the one of Pliny at the cathedral of Como, but in that cathedral on the day after his inauguration in 2011, the then bishop of Albany preached: "Ultimate victory over forces that are seemingly insurmountable is really possible." According to the *New York Daily News*: "The divorced son of former Gov. Mario Cuomo, who was once chastised by Catholic leaders for his support of abortion rights, calmly received Holy Communion. Lee walked in line for Communion with him." Immediately after the Mass, Cuomo the Younger said that the bishop's words were "inspirational" and then ordered ethics training for employees in his office, to be given by the Public Integrity Commission. One supposes that such training includes eradicating the superstitious cult of Christianity.

Attributed to Alexis de Tocqueville, but more probably the words of Joseph de Maistre, is the oft-repeated warning, "In a democracy, people get the government they deserve." New York now has the highest abortion rate in the nation, and Governor Cuomo promotes abortion even in the third trimester when a baby can feel pain, and apparently more so than the governor himself. In a state whose population supposedly is 38 percent Catholic, he enjoys a 52 percent approval record and received 61 percent of the nominal Catholic vote. Catholics fragile in spirit who symbolically offered incense to Caesar by voting for such present leaders were either ignorant (and ignorance unlike stupidity

can be cured) or selfish in placing small material interests above moral
standards.

Trajan was a comparatively humane man by the standards of the day,
but he seems to have been inflated with his successes against the Scythi-
ans and Dacians and became more bloated with pride when he decided
to march on Armenia. According to tradition, en route to Armenia,
Trajan stopped in Antioch, where the bishop Ignatius was brought
before him. Trajan was perplexed that such a gentle man would not
water down his faith in order to cooperate with the State. He ordered
Ignatius to get out of Bythinia. Before arriving in Rome, where he
was tossed to the lions by imperial decree, Saint Ignatius wrote: "Do
not err, my brethren. Those that corrupt families shall not inherit the
kingdom of God. If, then, those who do this as respects the flesh have
suffered death, how much more shall this be the case with any one
who corrupts by wicked doctrine the faith of God, for which Jesus
Christ was crucified! Such a one becoming defiled [in this way], shall
go away into everlasting fire and so shall every one that hearkens unto
him."

Saint Ignatius was second in succession to Saint Peter as bishop of
Antioch, after the death of Bishop Evodius, and he may have been
appointed by the Prince of the Apostles himself. He was a student of
Christ's most beloved apostle John. So what Ignatius wrote resounds
with the authority Christ gave to Peter and resonates with the beat of
the heart John could hear at the Last Supper.

22

WHAT'S IN A NAME?

THE MONTAGUES AND CAPULETS placed great store in their brand names, even to the point of stabbing one another, but the Capulet girl was a wistful voice: "What's in a name? That which we call a rose / By any other name would smell as sweet."

Move from that miserable imbroglio in Verona across a few centuries to the United States, and the tension persists, especially among cranks whose affectation of being scandalized for personal gain outdoes the least righteous of the Pharisees. Ignorance of etymology fuels the fire of such people, and consequently there is the foolishness of banning the term "tar baby" from storybooks even though it has nothing to do with race. It is like an untutored man who is shocked to hear that his daughter has matriculated in public on her first day at college. There is the actual instance of the forced resignation of a mayoral aide in Washington, D.C., for using the word "niggardly" with reference to the city budget. A member of the city council who objected that the term was racist was weak in his grasp of the Old Norse origin of the root word *nigla*, which means "fussing pedantically over nonsense".

Things got complicated when the shocked city councilman was called "homophobic" by members of the "gay community", which defended the mayoral aide as one of their own. Even the good word "gay" has become freighted with new meaning, and I expect that the Gordon Highlanders may next object that the Scottish folkdance the "Gay Gordons" has become misinterpreted. This is not helped by the

Originally published in *Crisis Magazine*, November 6, 2013.

fact that it is danced counterclockwise. Julian Bond, as head of the NAACP, an organization that has managed steadfastly to keep its official name, sensibly said of the niggardly incident: "You hate to think that you have to censor your language to meet other people's lack of understanding."

There was real lack of understanding behind complaints about the trademarked name of the Washington Redskins professional football team as racist and demeaning. That was shot down in District Court and the Court of Appeals, and finally in 2009 the U.S. Supreme Court declined to hear the case. One of the original complaints came from a Native American who was one year old when "Redskins" was registered as a mark in 1967. I myself have no case against calling Native Americans "Native Americans", and I am well aware that the Lenni-Lenape were tilling the land on which I was born for possibly eleven centuries before my natal day. In 1684 a Scots settler, perhaps a Gordon for all we know, said they were "gentle, kind and good". That was in New Jersey, and anyone born in New Jersey is radically native to America, so I claim the name for myself as well.

Now the case against the Washington Redskins has been revived, and it is an echo of stirrings from the 1970s, when a group of "college activists" forced Dartmouth to change its symbol from an Indian to a Pine Tree, even though pine trees lack athletic prowess. At the time, to the embarrassment of mostly pale-faced campus "activists", chiefs of tribes across the nation said in a survey that they wanted to keep the Indian. Dartmouth was chartered by King George III in 1769 "for the education & instruction of Youth of the Indian tribes in this Land in reading, writing & all parts of Learning which shall appear necessary and expedient for civilizing & christianizing Children of Pagans as well as in all liberal Arts and Sciences; and also of English Youth and any others."

The King refers to "savage" tribes, as would the Declaration of Independence, protesting that His Majesty had allied the "merciless Indian savages" against the English in the colonies. The problem was not savagery but mercilessness. "Savage" is not a high compliment and certainly can be pejorative, but it is properly understood with detachment in the sense of its Latin source *silvaticus*, meaning wandering and wild, which would apply today to the typical undergraduate, whose vocabulary is much more limited than that of any of the Algonquian language groups.

In this there was nothing racist, for categorization according to color took hold more tenaciously and systematically only among the Rationalists of the late eighteenth century and subsequent Social Darwinists. Jefferson himself extolled the integrity and potential of Indian culture in his "Notes on the State of Virginia", to which he appended a speech of the Mingo chief Logan lamenting the destruction of his family by a white settler, as comparable to anything in classical or modern oratory. Recent scholarship has argued that "Redskin" was a rare usage before the nineteenth century and referred not to race, but to war paint designating strength and bravery, rather the way the head of the Society of Jesus is called the "Black Pope" because he wears black and not because of his skin. But now we have a Jesuit pope who wears white, so that muddles things.

The term "Redskin" was a translation of the *Peau-Rouge* neologism of the benign and longsuffering French Jesuit missionaries. It was also self-referential, and the chief of the Sauks, Quashquame, was recorded in 1825 as referring to his "Red Skin nation". In novels such as *The Pioneers* two years before the quotation of Quashquame, and *Last of the Mohicans*, a year later, James Fenimore Cooper popularized the term in allusion to native people he thought "comely" and never as an insult. Not infrequently did various sachems refer to Europeans as "red men" because of how they were sunburned by an unfamiliar outdoor life.

If we want to play social engineers with the names of sports teams, we shall catch a host of problems worldwide. Consider some of the names of teams: Albania—*Kuqezinjte* (the red and black); Rwanda—*Amavubi* (Wasps); Poland—*Bialo-Czerwoni* (white and red). It may be that there is not a majority of Irishmen now among Notre Dame's "Fighting Irish", but that is a stereotype if ever there was one. No team calls itself the "Fighting Anglo-Saxons". Then there are the "Ragin' Cajuns" at the University of Louisiana at Lafayette, and the prospect of the Minnesota "Vikings" ever taking on the Hawaiian "Rainbows" conjures overwhelming carnage. Worse would be the Penn "Quakers" up against Yeshiva University's "Maccabees". Christendom College has the "Crusaders", which would please King Louis IX, if not President Obama, who has suggested whitewashing the Washington Redskins, although he subsequently welcomed to the White House the NHL champions, the Chicago Blackhawks. It is nice to know that the cerebral New Jersey Institute of Technology manages to field a team called the "Highlanders". There loom the problematic Gordons again.

We have not yet reached the nadir of the Nika Riots in Justinian's Constantinople in 532. The city was as sports crazy as we are, which is always a sign of decadence, and the Hippodrome was right next to the royal palace so that the emperor could watch the races at home before the days of television. His wife, Theodora, was a sports fan even more fanatical than Justinian and helped stoke the violence that destroyed much of the city including that greatest of churches, Hagia Sophia. The teams were harmlessly named the Blue and the Green, but they came to represent political parties and, worse, theological parties, for the Blues were orthodox believers while the Greens were Monophysite heretics. Politics and religion played out in the circus was a volatile combination, and about thirty thousand were killed in one of the worst riots in history.

What, then, is in a name? I refer to our Lord, who says: "To him who conquers I will give some of the hidden manna, and I will give him a white stone, with a new name written on the stone which no one knows except him who receives it" (Rev 2:17). One theory is that since Jesus is speaking here to the Church in Pergamum, this is an allusion to the temple of Asclepius, on whose marble pillars were carved the names of those healed there, rather like votives in Lourdes and Fatima. More likely, it is sourced in the custom of ancient Rome to give the winner of a contest a white stone inscribed with his name as an admission ticket to the victory banquet.

All of our games are foolish unless they are understood as intimations of the great race that is set before us which is life itself. It is so ardent a run and so ennobling an adventure, that to sully it with silly politics and mindless bias is to risk the prize of the heavenly city where all the tribes go up. So, dear Juliet Capulet, it would seem that there is much in a name, and all depends on him at whose name every knee should bend.

23

HAIR OF THE HEIR

THE BIRTH OF Prince George Alexander Louis of Cambridge on July 22, 2013, stirred up much celebrating, save for a few curmudgeons like Vladimir Zhirinovsky, leader of Russia's Liberal Democratic Party, who rather excessively predicted that the little prince would "suck the blood" of the Russian people by the middle of this century. Choice of the name George was particularly gratifying to those under the patronage of that saint. He may well be the patron of more nations, provinces, and institutions than any saint save our Lady. The removal of Saint George to a third-class minor saint by Pope Paul VI in 1963 was undone by Pope John Paul II, when he restored him to the universal calendar and gave him special first-class rank in England and India. George is the baptismal name of Pope Francis, and so April 23 will have special resonance during his reign.

Most iconography shows Saint George with thick curly hair, which is strange since his demotion in 1963 was because supposedly little is known about him. Little Prince George Alexander Louis, like many babies, even royal ones, came into the world with fine but sparse hair. Some of the press occupied airtime remarking that his father is balding. This is also the case with Prince William's uncle, Prince Edward. Prince Harry has thick red hair, encouraging gossips to claim that he is not royal at all. Prince George's maternal great grandfather, the eighth Earl Spencer, was pretty thin on top, as were the second Earl and his youngest son, the Venerable Ignatius Spencer, a Catholic convert and

Originally published in *Crisis Magazine*, July 26, 2013.

Passionist priest. Father Spencer collapsed and died in a ditch in 1864 in consummation of arduous preaching and begging for the poor.

The Queen has great hair, and, being monarch of all she surveys and titular head of two billion people, she does not have any need to change styles. The first Elizabeth went bald and had at least eighty wigs, but she was a queen and not a king, and bald queens are not as handsome as bald kings. Louis XIII regretted his hair loss and affected wigs, and they became the fashion for a long time. Emperor Joseph abolished them as court dress in 1780, but the final blow was the French Revolution, when wigs were disdained as aristocratic symbols, and soon the guillotine saw to it that there were no heads to put them on. In the early days of the Church they were condemned as vanities: Saint Cyprian said that wearing a wig was worse than committing adultery, and Saint Clement of Alexandria held that when a blessing was given, it was blocked by the wig and did not reach the soul. Bishop Synesius, bishop of Ptolemais in the Libyan Pentapolis who died ca. 414, discoursed on the advantages of baldness as did the Frankish Benedictine monk Hucbald (d. 930) in his "Ecloga de Calvis". Synesius was something of an eccentric as well as a heretic and contradicted himself by admiring Hypatia, who was famous for her long hair. Nonetheless, he was at least as brilliant as Hucbald, whose "Ecloga", dedicated to the bald archbishop of Mainz, merits a decent place in the treasury of acrostics written in hexameter verse. In the eighteenth century, Clement XI forbade the wearing of wigs by local Roman clergy in the provincial councils of 1701 and 1706, and Benedict XIII ordered Cardinal Alberoni out of a procession for wearing one, but courtiers could wear them. Benedict XIV mitigated the strictures in 1725, and understandably so since he wore one in winter months. Curiously, wigs assumed an almost liturgical significance in the Church of England and were required for official acts; there was a special design for the clerical wig, as there were for those worn by barristers and judges. In the early nineteenth century in New York, a question arose among Episcopalians about the validity of their bishops consecrated without wigs.

As for the hair of the Windsors, the roots go back well into Saxon mists, assuming that the most common form of male pattern baldness, androgenic alopecia, is hereditary. This genetic tradition is, according to experts, "autosomal dominant with mixed penetrance". I quote that without comment, since I do not know what it means, but I do know that bald royals tend to beget bald royals here and there. In the present case of the Mountbatten-Windsors, one might check out the Count of Flanders, Baudouin II, born in 864, who passed the gene through the Princess Elfrida of Wessex. The present alopeciac Prince Edward is Earl of Wessex.

In the ninth century, King Aethelwulf of Wessex, who actually had been born in Aachen, was a man of deep piety. He sent his four-year-old son Alfred to Rome laden with petitionary prayers in 853 and joined him two years later, showering the pope with lavish gifts of gold vessels and silver candelabra of fine Saxon craftsmanship. In the course of his return, he visited the court of the king of the western Franks, Charles the Bald. There he married Charles' twelve-year-old daughter, Judith of Flanders, his first wife Osburh having died.

Aethelwulf had five sons and a daughter. The eldest, Aethelstan, was killed by the Vikings in what is considered Britain's first naval battle. The second son, ambitious Aethelbald, had already taken over some of his father's lands and when Aethelwulf died in 858, he became King of all Wessex and also wed his stepmother Judith. Upon the deaths of his brothers Aethelberht and Aethelred, kings in their own turn, Alfred —known to posterity as the Great—acceded to the throne. The new king commissioned a book of charms, that is, Latin verses describing medical cures, which had been passed along to him by Elias, the Patriarch of Jerusalem. An extant version of the book is called "Bald's Leechbook" for its owner, mentioned in a colophon at the end of the Leechbook: "Bald habet hunc librum Cild quem conscribere iussit (Bald is the owner of this book which he ordered Cild to compile)." In early Anglo-Saxon usage, "bald" meant bold or courageous, and only gradually in Middle English did it come to mean a lack of hair. The Welsh equivalent for bold is "ddewr", and the word for bald is "foel". When the Saxon king Aethelstan took the throne in 924, he joined forces against the Scots with the Welsh ruler Idwal Foel (Idwal the Bald) but as that alliance ended on the death of Aethelstan, it cannot be proven that any genetic trait was passed through a royal marriage. The present Prince of Wales is thinning, appropriately, on the crown of his head.

Fast forwarding through the royal ages, androgenic alopecia cropped up in the reign of George III. His tenth child, Prince Adolphus, Duke of Cambridge, was totally bald and became the uncle of Queen Victoria, who married the prematurely balding Prince Albert. Prince Adolphus was also, through the Württemburg line, the grandfather of Mary of Teck, who became the queen consort of George V and the present Queen's grandmother. Queen Mary's brother took the name of his great great uncle as first Marquess of Cambridge and, as can be seen in a chromolithograph by Sir Leslie Ward, was bald at an early age.

One wishes the best for every baby, and it is certainly hoped that the newborn Prince George will not be like Absalom, the princely son of King David, with hair so long that it got caught in the branches of a terebinth tree, leading to his death. What the Bible teaches us about all this is left for dispassionate exegetes to tell. We do know that God's judgments are severe against those whose sense of humor is so primitive that they resort to telling bald jokes. A crowd of boys jeered at the prophet Elisha on his way to Bethel, shouting: "Go up, you baldhead! Go up, you baldhead!" The prophet cursed them in the name of the Lord. "And two she-bears came out of the woods and tore forty-two of the boys" (2 Kings 2:24). The meaning of this edifying scene is for those wise enough to understand.

24

THE MORAL EXPLOITATION OF PENGUINS

O F ALL GOD'S CREATURES, those most amiable must include koalas, pandas, dolphins, and penguins, only the last two of which are aquatic. If one goes with most evolutionists, penguins used to fly, and flying would have made it easier to escape their chief enemy the leopard seal, but their ability to swim made flying too much of an effort, and gradually their wings became attenuated. Perhaps the closest we have today to the last of the flying penguins is the pelagic cormorants (*Phalacrocorax pelagicus*), and they seem to have retained their soaring ability only by swimming with their feet. Emperor penguins can quickly dive to 1,500 feet using their former wings that became flippers, and isotope analysis of how they burn energy indicates that such consumption exhausted the biomechanical energy for flying. This is true of all penguins. Of the seventeen species of penguins, just four breed on the Antarctic continent: the Adelie, the Emperor, and the Chinstrap among them. The largest species is the Macaroni penguin, which Australian ornithologists tend to lump together with the Royal Penguin, reducing the number of species to sixteen. One respected study numbers the Macaronis at 11,654,000 pairs, and the amateur can only wonder at how this was calculated and at what cost to the social lives of those who counted them.

It is the Chinstrap penguin (*Pygoscelis antarctica*) on which we are focused. Wherever you find them: Antarctica, South Shetland, South Georgia, Bouvet Island, Deception Island, or the sunnier South Sandwich Islands, their distinctive black band around the necks cannot be

Originally published in *Crisis Magazine*, July 15, 2013.

missed, and hence their name. Depending on their breeding cycle, their weight can drop from more than thirteen pounds to between six and seven pounds, and breeding is the issue here. While my contempt for the unfitting things that *The New York Times* prints is not effortlessly concealed, I was especially exercised by the way that declining journal has over the years used dolphins and other creatures, including the Chinstrap penguin, to promote an antinomian theory that unnatural sexual activity is okay. Specifically, I allude to its article published on February 7, 2004, under the belabored title, "Love That Dare Not Squeak Its Name". First of all, penguins do not "squeak". That is the sort of stereotyping that *The New York Times* generally eschews, save in the instances of supply-side economists, black conservatives, and practicing Christians. Penguins make various sounds: the African, Humboldt, Galapagos, and Magellanic penguins make a braying sound very much like donkeys, while the Yellow-eyed penguin trills, the King penguin sounds like a trumpet, and our immediate concern, the Chinstrap, has a shrill voice almost like a scream. None of them, dear editors of *The New York Times*, squeaks. A simple trip to the Central Park Zoo would confirm this, and if those editors had made the trip, they would not have made their big mistake: the announcement that some Chinstrap penguins are homosexual.

Polemicists exaggerate statistics as a matter of policy, and *The New York Times* devotes its front page, "Style Section", and even obituaries to creating the illusion that there are far more "non-heterosexuals" than there really are. Like the quest for the "gay gene", which, like the "missing link", is, as Chesterton pointed out, missing, a constant effort is afoot to find rampant unnatural activity in nature to justify it as a norm. This is why "The Grey Lady" (or "The Grey Person") trumpeted like a King penguin a claim that two male Chinstrap penguins at the Central Park Zoo were attracted to each other. The article claimed that Roy and Silo had been inseparable for nearly six years and rubbed their necks in "ecstatic behavior". More than that, they eschewed female companionship. Their chief keeper, Rob Gramzay, claimed that they tried to incubate a rock. When, as expected, this did not work, he gave them a fertile egg, which hatched after Roy and Silo sat on it for thirty-four days. *The New York Times* seems to have inferred from this a lesson in surrogate parenthood. Roy and Silo fed their chick, named Tango, until she could manage on her own. As the paper of record noted, "Mr. Gramzay is full of praise for them." In a later article (September 24, 2015), Mr. Gramzay "never saw the pair complete a sex act, though the two did engage in mating rituals like entwining their necks and vocalizing to one another".

Call it coincidence, but after news of Roy and Silo broke, homosexual penguins suddenly began to pop up all over the world. Newspapers in Toronto reported the amorous activities of African penguins Buddy and Pedro in their local zoo, although Buddy seems to have been bisexual as evidenced in his quick surrender to the affections of a female penguin named Farai. Almost exactly one year after the startling announcement in *The New York Times* about Roy and Silo, the Bremerhaven Zoo disclosed that it had tried but failed to split up three homosexual pairs of penguins by introducing them to some females of the same species imported from Sweden. Zoo director Heike Kueck declared this "aversion therapy" a disappointment and told a reporter that "All sorts of gay and lesbian associations have been e-mailing and calling in to protest." Penguins had become a symbol of their struggle for gender neutrality. Not to be outdone, scientists at Tokyo's Rikkyo University listed about twenty same-sex pairs in sixteen zoos in Japan. As the Scandinavian lands have been more libertine in sexual taxonomy, it is no surprise that keepers in the Odense Zoo in Denmark disclosed that two homosexual male penguins had tried to steal eggs from mother penguins and even went to the extreme of attempting to incubate a dead herring. London's *Daily Mail* then ran an account of Inca and Rayas, two male penguins at Faunia Park in Madrid who had maintained a relationship exactly the same length of time as the prototypical Roy and Silo in New York.

As members of the animal kingdom share with man to some degree the consequences of a fallen world, their behavior should not be taken as a model of prelapsarian perfection. If, citing Cole Porter, even educated fleas do it, doing it a different way does not make it a right way. Even poor little lambs go astray. Either accept that to go astray is not right, or you have to say that no one strays. A few years ago in the San Diego zoo, an orangutan was upset by a woman's hat and threw his own excrement at it. This does not make him an arbiter of fashion, nor should dissolute penguins be cited as evidence in moral discourse.

Within months after *The New York Times* scooped the tabloids on what was going on in the Central Park penguin pavilion, Peter Parnell and Justin Richardson wrote a book about Roy and Silo for children entitled *And Tango Makes Three*. According to one review, "The book follows the six years of their life when they formed a couple and were given an egg to raise." It received many awards from groups that apparently look to penguins as moral templates. According to the American Library Association, *And Tango Makes Three* was the most "challenged" book of 2006, 2007, and 2008 and returned to the top rank in 2010. In Shiloh, Illinois, a school superintendent rejected parents' pleas that the book be put in a restricted area of the library. However, the book was banned in Singapore. On October 2, 2009, *The New York Times* announced that, "as life imitates art", Parnell and Richardson "have their own baby Tango. In February, the gay couple, who live in the West Village, had their first child. The baby, Gemma Parnell-Richardson, was born to a surrogate mother, the egg fertilized by sperm from one of the men. (Which one was left to chance.)" Thus they were spared the indignity of trying to incubate a rock or a dead herring.

As an aside, naming the baby penguin for the tango dance unwittingly brings up another moral controversy. In 1913 the Kaiser condemned the tango, for fear of its effects on his Crown Princess. More pertinent to the theological aspect, is Pope Saint Pius X's informal condemnation of the tango after he had watched an exhibition performance at the request of Cardinal Merry del Val, who thought the Pontiff might approve a sober version of it as choreographed by the Roman dance master Professor Pichetti. The pope was not impressed and recommended instead the "Furlana", an Italian folk dance that goes back to the early seventeenth century in Friuli Venezia Giulia and with which he had been familiar in his youth. This papal objurgation of the tango continued until the recent election of the first Argentinian pope, when it actually was danced in Saint Peter's Square on the pope's birthday. It would be a "reduction ad absurdum" to think that this has any bearing on the penguin hatchling Tango as a cipher for the development of moral doctrine, but the publicity of its birth further increased polemics until, alas, proponents of Roy and Silo learned that soon after the birth of Tango, Silo abandoned Roy for a female Chinstrap from California named Scrappy.

A history professor at Yale, John Boswell, was a convert to Roman Catholicism and died in 1994 from AIDS related complications at the age of forty-seven, having spent much of his career arguing that the

Church had sanctioned "adelphopoiesis" as a rite uniting two person of the same sex in a romantic and sexual bond. His critics pointed out the many flaws in his thesis, most importantly his misinterpretation of the traditions of fraternity and "blood brotherhood". He used iconography, such as images of Saints Sergius and Bacchus, as evidence for his propaganda, rather the way journalists have used penguins. All of them nimbly ignored the Fathers such as Saint John Chrysostom, who probably had never seen a penguin but who wrote in his fourth Commentary on the Epistle to the Romans that not even wild animals go beyond the boundaries of a male uniting with a female, or what the sixteenth canon of the Council of Ancyra in 314 called "doing the irrational" (*alogeuesthai*).

After its intrusion into the domestic manners of Roy and Silo, *The New York Times* printed a correction on February 23, 2004: "A picture in Arts & Ideas on Feb. 7 with an article about homosexual behavior in animals, including bottlenose dolphins, was published in error. It showed killer whales." This does not increase our confidence in the newspaper, nor does it make the chaste swimmer eager to go far from the beach.

25

A CATHOLIC CURIOSITY:
THE LIFE OF SIR JEFFREY HUDSON

S HAKESPEARE'S HENRY V OFFERS THIS ADVICE: "This story shall the good man teach his son." Such counsel is urgent today, when children will learn little reliably of their history in schools and so are all the more dependent on good souls at home who will teach them. Children, being children, will especially be fascinated by curiosities. Although I may not have been representative of all children in my own youth, one of my earliest fascinations was with Norse migrations to Vinland in the eleventh century and, in particular, the controversial Kensington Runestone dug up in Minnesota. Oddities like that tend to rivet a child's imagination and would be helpful for interesting the fathers of the next generation in the fathers of their past.

A boy's eyes may glaze over if he is made to memorize only names and dates, but tell him something odd about those names and dates and it will never be forgotten. Consider, as one case in point, the defeat of the Scots by the Moors at Teba near Málaga on their way to bury the heart of Robert the Bruce in Jerusalem. King Robert had been excommunicated by both Pope Clement V and Pope John XXII, and the burial of his heart in the Holy Land was to be a penitential gesture, entrusted to Sir James Douglas. When he was killed at Teba on August 25, 1330, the knight William Keith of Galston brought it back to Melrose Abbey in Scotland. Some 201 years earlier, the heart of Richard the Lionheart was buried in Rouen, embalmed with frankincense, as were his entrails, which were entombed at Châlus, and the

Originally published in *Crisis Magazine*, June 10, 2013.

rest of his body at Fontevraud Abbey in Anjou. The same John XXII who excommunicated the Bruce had received favorably in 1320 the Declaration of Arbroath, which contained many expressions anticipatory of our 1776 Declaration of Independence. Its reputed author, Abbot Bernard, may thus be called the Thomas Jefferson of Scotland. Or, more fittingly, Thomas Jefferson was the Abbot Bernard of the United States. Arbroath had a happier connection with the papacy than did Magna Carta, which Pope Innocent III called "a shameful and demeaning agreement forced upon the King by violence and fear". At least the pope could read the Latin document. In a recent interview on American television, British Prime Minister David Cameron was unable to translate the words "Magna Carta". That does not speak well of his schooling at Eton and Oxford. Perhaps his father should have spent more time teaching him at home.

In the saga of Catholic curiosities, unique is the smallest known adult Catholic, Sir Jeffrey Hudson, who as a man was eighteen inches tall. His parents and siblings were of average height. He was not a typical dwarf, inasmuch as he was perfectly proportioned in every way, only tiny—more of what is called vernacularly a midget, and technically a pituitary dwarf, conditioned by a lack of growth hormone. But his hypopituitarism was without precedent in England, and his perfect and delicate miniature size distinguished him from the common Continental court dwarves of his day. It might be noted here that as plurals, dwarfs and dwarves seem to be legitimate options—Tolkien popularized the latter, while the former was the traditional form and was preferred by C. S. Lewis. I suppose the two writers had little disagreement over it at the height of their popularity, but the long and short of it is that they agreed to disagree about so tiny a matter, and their literary merit dwarfs any minor question about spelling.

As a possible portent, Hudson was born on June 14, 1619, in England's smallest county, Rutland, whose motto is "Multum in Parvo", or, Much in Little, as David Cameron might try to translate it. His father raised cattle, particularly bulls for baiting, for the Duke of Buckingham. When little Jeffrey failed to grow, he was taken into the Buckingham household as a "rarity of nature". He was seven years old, and when King Charles I and his queen Henrietta Maria were entertained by the Duke and Duchess of Buckingham, the lavish banquet ended with a large pie out of which popped Jeffrey Hudson in a miniature suit of armor. This gave rise to a rumor that he had been baked in the pie, but this was not the case. The Queen was so delighted that the Buckinghams presented their rarity to her. The Queen kept a separate household at Denmark House in London, and Jeffrey joined it at the end of 1626, along with two disproportionate dwarfs and a Welsh giant. Jeffrey became favored for his wit and elegance, and Inigo Jones wrote costumed masques in which he played small parts. The French queen's court was Catholic and housed so many priests that some objections were raised among Londoners who feared a conspiracy might be afoot. Jeffrey embraced Catholicism and kept his faith throughout his difficult life, regularly assisting at Low Masses, which occasioned tasteless puns.

In 1630, ten-year-old Jeffrey was sent to the French court to accompany a midwife back to England for the Queen. His returning ship was seized by Dunkirk pirates, but he was saved and crossed the Channel again in 1637 to watch the siege of Breda, which the Dutch fought against the Spanish. Back in England, he became an accomplished horseman, with a special saddle, and in the heat of the Civil War he was made a "Captain of Horse" when the royal family was billeted in Oxford and soon was knighted by King Charles I, though Sir Jeffrey preferred the title Captain as he aspired to greater heights. It was better than his court nickname, Lord Minimus. He accompanied the Queen to the Netherlands in 1642 to raise money for the Royalist troops, although the Dutch Protestants would not promise public support. He went with the Queen when she fled to France, living briefly in the Louvre and then removing with the Queen's court to Nevers. There he made his big mistake. For some unknown reason he got into a heated argument with the brother of William Crofts, the Queen's Master of Horse. Very likely, Sir Jeffrey had repulsed an insult about his physical size. By this time, he had assumed a dignity of carriage and sense of importance and no longer would be the court plaything. He was a man, and a man of stature if not of height. So he challenged his small-minded offender to a duel. His opponent thought the challenge of tiny Jeffrey ridiculous and said so. Since by force of circumstance he could not box without hitting below the belt, Jeffrey chose to duel with pistols on horseback. Crofts mocked him by showing up with two water pistols. Sir Jeffrey Hudson rode toward him on his horse and shot him in the head, killing him instantly. As dueling was banned in France, his residency was cut short and he was expelled from court and country.

By this time he was twenty-five and set sail only to be kidnapped by Barbary pirates. His Muslim captors took him to North Africa, where he labored as a slave for twenty-five years. With the restoration of the English monarchy, numerous attempts were made to release slaves in Tunisia and Algeria. Hudson was among those rescued. In response to a brief submitted on his behalf, since he had fallen short in payments on numerous debt obligations, he received a small pension from the new Duke of Buckingham, son of his first benefactor, and from Charles II. While Hudson's first king was only 4′8″ tall (slightly taller in his shoes with red high heels, which were the fashion of royalty), Charles II was 6′2″, perhaps a throwback to his great grandmother Mary, Queen of Scots, who was six feet tall. Curiously, in his years of slavery, Jeffrey had grown in spurts to 48 inches, which is not uncommon for those with pituitary deficiency, so he could no longer make much of a living as a curiosity, since he now looked like a small boy rather than a woodland sprite. Nor would he have wanted to, given his self-respect and accomplishments. Unfortunately, his return to England was co-incident with anti-Catholic hysteria attendant upon the plot of Titus Oates, who had been born in Hudson's native town of Oakham, and so he managed to keep a low profile. He did give some lengthy interviews and returned to London from Oakham in 1676, when he was quickly imprisoned at the Gatehouse prison for "being a Roman Catholick". He died two years after his release in 1680 in reduced circumstances, but the date of his death is unknown, and he was buried as a pauper in an unmarked grave.

Sir Walter Scott mentions him in one of his Waverley novels, *Peveril of the Peak*, and some of his clothing, including a blue velvet court dress, is preserved at Sherborne castle in Dorset. In the Second World War, that castle housed the commandoes preparing for the D-Day invasion, which would have pleased Sir Jeffrey (sometimes spelled Jeffery), who landed on the French beaches more than once. The gardens of Sherborne were much admired by Alexander Pope, who rejoiced in such a Catholic name although he was only a second-generation Catholic. That poet, as the result of disease of the spinal cord, was four feet tall, the same size as Jeffrey upon his return from North Africa. It is fascinating to think that Pope could have fit into Jeffrey's clothes, at least those of his later period. For some unclear reason, a life-sized statue of England's littlest knight is in the public bar of the Boat Inn in Portumna, County Galway. A marker near his birthplace bears the singular inscription:

"Sir Jeffery Hudson—1619–1682—A dwarf presented in a pie to King Charles 1st." And this story shall the good man teach his son.

26

ABBÉ EDGEWORTH

A MONG THE SINGULARITIES of the French monarchy was the tradition of having Scottish bodyguards. Scottish history has not been
riddled with pacifism, and the Scots along with the fiery Castilians
were used as mercenaries as early as Charlemagne. An "Auld Alliance"
between Scotland and France was sealed in 1295, and in the dark war
days of 1942, Charles de Gaulle invoked it as "the oldest alliance in
the world". In 1418, as Charles VI began to go mad, the Dauphin
called on Scottish troops to support his cause against Henry V. They
were victorious at the battle of Baugé in 1421, prompting Pope Martin V to comment: "The Scots are well known as an antidote to the
English." Saint Joan of Arc entered besieged Orleans in 1429 with a
retinue of 130 Scots guards protecting her and playing on bagpipes the
same tune, "Hey Tuttie Taiti", that had been played for Robert the
Bruce at the Battle of Bannockburn a century before. The guards and
pipers were also present with Joan at the coronation of the Dauphin as
Charles VII at Rheims. The new king chose one hundred of the Scots
as his personal bodyguards to honor their heroism when six thousand
of their number died at the Battle of Verneuil in 1424. The "Garde
Ecossaise" later became the "Gardes de la Manche", since they escorted
the king close enough to be touched by his sleeve. By the eighteenth
century, some of them were more French than Scottish, but they wore
the thistle and carried claymores with basket guards of steel, guarding
the French kings until Charles X abdicated in the July Revolution of

Originally published in *Crisis Magazine*, May 15, 2013.

1830. They served as a poignant reminder of the Auld Alliance, which lasted until 1906, and as late as then, anyone born in Scotland could have dual citizenship with France.

This recalls another Celtic curiosity: the priest who accompanied King Louis XVI to his execution was Irish. Rarely does anyone ask why the French king had an Irish confessor. Like the Garde Ecossaise, there is of course an explanation, and an edifying one at that.

Henry Essex Edgeworth was born in County Longford at Firmont, the ancestral home of the Edgeworths, who had come from Middlesex, England, during the reign of Elizabeth in 1582. In their house, Oliver Goldsmith had learned to read and write. Henry was a great-grandson, through his maternal line, of Archbishop James Ussher, the seventeenth-century Anglican Primate of Ireland, who was a first-rate classicist but a less distinguished historian, as he used the date of King Nebuchadnezzar's death to calculate that the world was created on October 23, 4004 B.C. His contemporary John Lightfoot, Vice-Chancellor of Cambridge University, outdid him by dating the expulsion of Adam and Eve from Eden at 10 A.M. on Monday, November 10 in the same year. Just as Edgeworth eventually would do, Ussher witnessed the execution of his sovereign (from the roof of Lady Peterborough's house) but fainted before the axe was brought down.

Henry's mother, Martha, was the daughter of Christopher Ussher of Wicklow, an unyielding Protestant who wrote in his Last Will: "My daughters Catherine Ussher and Martha Edgeworth are turned Roman Catholiques and have quitted me and my family and all natural ties to them and their country. I leave them one shilling each, with my blessing." Henry's father, Robert, was an Anglican clergyman whose own family was not unfriendly to Catholics. One of them recalled: "The Roman Catholic Bishop M'Gaurin, held a Confirmation the day before yesterday, and dined here on a God-send haunch of venison." The Reverend Robert Edgeworth made an intense profession of the Catholic faith and left the Penal Laws behind for France with his wife, his sister-in-law Catherine, and his youngest son, Henry, who began studies in Toulouse and eventually was ordained in Paris. He had hoped to become a foreign missionary and lived at the residence of Les Missions étrangères, working with all ranks of the agitated populace, gaining a great following among the poorest, and counseling expatriate English and Irish, converting some Protestants among them. He chose not to accept the offer of a bishopric back in Ireland so that he might minister to the poor Savoyards of Paris. At the outbreak of the Revolution, the Archbishop of Paris, Monsignor Antoine Le Clerc de Juigné, nominated him as confessor to Madame Elisabeth, the sister of Louis XVI, and he visited her frequently in prison. His mother and sister joined him in Paris, his mother eventually dying in captivity while his sister died later. The archbishop gave the Abbé Henri Essex Edgeworth de Firmont the title Grand Vicaire, with responsibility for all the Catholics of Paris, and fled for his own life to Germany. An aunt in Galway asked him to flee and be her chaplain, as she had also become Catholic, but he excused himself, saying that his English had become poor after many years abroad. A letter to a priest in London told the truth:

> Almighty God has baffled my measures, and ties me to this land of horrors by chains I have not the liberty to shake off. The case is this: the wretched master [the king] charges me not to quit this country, as I am the priest whom he intends to prepare him for death. And should the iniquity of the nation commit this last act of cruelty, I must also prepare myself for death, as I am convinced the popular rage will not allow me to survive an hour after the tragic scene; but I am resigned. Could my life save him I would willingly lay it down, and I should not die in vain.

The evening before January 21, 1793, the Abbé fell in tears at the king's feet. Louis helped him up, made his last confession, and then bade farewell to the queen and their children. The Commune having reluctantly allowed the Abbé to put on vestments, as clerical dress had been forbidden, he said Mass and gave the king his last Communion. The two stayed together until dawn:

> The King, finding himself seated in the carriage, where he could neither speak to me nor be spoken to without witness, kept a profound silence. I presented him with my breviary, the only book I had with me, and he seemed to accept it with pleasure: he appeared anxious that I should point out to him the psalms that were most suited to his situation, and he recited them attentively with me. The *gendarmes*, without speaking, seemed astonished and confounded at the tranquil piety of their monarch, to whom they doubtless never had before approached so near.[1]

---

[1] Henry Essex Edgeworth di Firmont, Charles Sneyd Edgeworth, *Memoirs of the Abbé Edgeworth* (Rowland Hunter, 1815), 79–80.

In one of his last gestures, the king placed his hand on Edgeworth's knee and then told the guard to take care of his priest. Louis appeared shocked when the guards began to bind his hands. Edgeworth told him: "Sire, in this new insult, I only see another trait of your Majesty and the Saviour who is about to recompense you." The youngest of the executioners, eighteen years old, held the king's head high and let some of the blood splatter on the Abbé. He slipped through the crowd: "All eyes were fixed on me, as you may believe; but as soon as I reached the first line, to my great astonishment, no resistance was made. . . . (I was not permitted, on this occasion, to wear any exterior marks of a priest), I was absolutely lost in the crowd, and no more noticed than if I had been a simple spectator of a scene, which for ever will dishonour France."

The Abbé first took refuge in the Rue du Bac, where the Blessed Mother would appear to Catherine Labouré in 1830. After a stay in Bayeux, he crossed to England in 1796 and went to Scotland to see the king's brother, the comte d'Artois. Prime Minister Pitt offered him a large pension, which he respectfully declined, along with the presidency of Maynooth seminary and honors from King Louis XVIII. He joined the exiled household of Louis in Blankenburg and moved with them to Mittau in Russia. Louis delegated him to go to Saint Petersburg and present the Order of the Holy Spirit to Czar Paul, who, moved by the transparent piety of Edgeworth, knelt and begged his blessing. Back in Mittau he contracted typhus from nursing sick French soldiers stranded during the Napoleonic campaign. Risking contagion, the Princess Marie-Thérèse, daughter of Louis XVI, attended the deathbed of the "beloved and revered invalid, her more than friend, who had left kindred and country for her family".

The Abbé Edgeworth never claimed to have said the words ascribed to him as the king climbed the steps to the guillotine, and many suppose they were as apocryphal as Newton's apple or the three hundred Spartans who stopped the army of Xerxes, but they were dear to Macaulay: "Enfant de Saint Louis, montez au ciel. Son of Saint Louis, climb up to heaven."

Louis XVIII did him the rare honor of personally composing his epitaph, and in splendid Latin, too:

Here lies the Very Reverend Henry Essex Edgeworth de Firmont; a priest of the Holy Church of God; Vicar-General of the Diocese of

Paris, etc., who, pursuing the steps of our Redeemer, was an eye to the blind, a staff to the lame, a father to the poor, and a consoler of the afflicted. When Louis XVI. was given up to death by his impious and rebellious subjects, he supported the resolute martyr in his last struggle, and pointed out to him the opening heavens. Snatched from the hands of the regicides by the wonderful protection of God, he voluntarily attached himself to Louis XVIII. when he signified his wish for his services. To whom, and to whose royal family and faithful household, he proved himself for a space of ten years, an example of virtue and an assuager of misfortune. Driven from kingdom to kingdom by the calamity of the times, he went about doing good, ever like to him who possessed his sole devotion. At length full of good-works, he died the 22d day of May, in the year of our Lord 1807, aged 62. *May he rest in peace.*

27

THE CHRISTIAN BOXER

W HEN OUR LORD SAYS turn the other cheek, he speaks of a spiritual strategy to humble the self and then, perhaps, to win other souls to him. He certainly was not counseling cowardice, and recent scriptural exegesis actually suggests that "turning the other cheek" means to be quick and agile enough to prevent an assailant from striking you a second time by rotating away from his right hand, which is his striking fist. When Cardinal Gibbons was a young pastor in Baltimore during the Civil War, according to his biographer, Allen Sinclair Wills, an irate soldier swung at him with a paling from the rectory fence, "he summoned his strength, knocked the man down and thoroughly subdued him. When the soldier came to his senses he realized that the frail young man in priestly dress was more than his match, and beat a precipitate retreat." But in the spiritual order, not all the proud are shamed by docile humility, and it seems pretty clear that those who smote the One who offered them salvation did not turn their hearts to him when he turned his cheek to them. Saint John Cantius won the hearts of some bandits when he called them back to take some money they had overlooked, but that is an instance rare enough to have become the lore of hagiography. Sane moralists insist that neglect of self-defense can be moral dereliction. Glad tidings of peace are not lighthearted pacifism, and even the Good Shepherd brought news to the poor and brokenhearted carrying a rod along with a staff. I learned the wisdom of this when I was briefly knocked unconscious by a man

Originally published in *Crisis Magazine*, April 8, 2013.

I had caught breaking into my church's Poor Box. It was then that I began instruction in boxing, which I still try to keep up about once a week.

My first coach was an African who hesitated to punch me. I told him I could never learn unless he punched me. He explained that in his homeland, superstitious people thought it bad luck to strike a priest. That is a superstition lacking in my own country.

The amateur boxer learns three things immediately. First, few activities are as physically demanding, and, at least in my case, one three-minute round can be more exhausting than running five miles. Second, boxing is highly intellectual, requiring so much quick reasoning and psychology that, of all sports, it is the one rightly called the "Sweet Science". Third, the immediate instinct to punch someone who has punched you issues in a thrill when you do so. When it is done gratuitously in sport, it can make one even less eager to do it in retributive anger. No one is disinterested in you once you have punched him, and so boxing with strangers can even create bonds of friendship.

That is not always the case, as we known from Ali's acid behavior toward Frazier outside the ring and from the famous brawl between Larry Holmes and Trevor Berbick, who later was murdered by his nephew, poignantly, in a church. Yet the saints themselves must have delighted in the way Gene Tunney and Jack Dempsey became lifelong friends after the notorious Long Count in 1927. Tunney's profits from the ring along with a beneficial marriage, by the way, enabled him to study literature, which he had not been able to do when poverty deprived him of school. The autodidact Tunney came to know Thornton Wilder and Ernest Hemingway, and he became the best of friends with George Bernard Shaw, once a bantamweight boxer himself. Tunney lectured on Shakespeare at Yale in its bright days.

Other sports such as baseball, tennis, and squash racquets have their place, but their common drawback is that their players get to strike each other only inadvertently. Football is as cerebral as boxing, but banging into one another is not as graceful as using fists. Then there are activities like shuffleboard, badminton, and billiards (and its outdoor variant: golf). As they have the advantage of being able to be played in a state of physical neglect or advanced pregnancy, they are games and not sports. Swimming is superb for health, of course, but the water required for it conceals any evidence of exertion. Fencing may match boxing for mental elegance, but the use of protective devices has made it a shadow of ancient duels. It is said that Saint Francis Xavier was a very good fencer and began fencing when he entered the Collège de Sainte-Barbe in Paris in 1525. Wrestling is the only real competition for boxing and is almost as ancient. While Cain boxed Abel with fatal results, wrestling only put Jacob's hip out of joint. If it is shockingly true that Greco-Roman and freestyle wrestling is to be dropped from the next Olympic games, which inexplicably include curling, ping pong, and beach volleyball, then the degradation of our culture has entered its fin-de-siècle phase of the Decadents.

Among sports, bullfighting is too rarefied to be considered here, though it has not escaped the attention of holy eyes. Pope Saint Pius V condemned it in 1567, but this may in part have been a reaction to the appetites of his Spanish Borgia antecedent. In 1597, Pope Clement VIII only forbade the clergy from attending or participating in bullfights, but this was little different from the policy against clerics attending the opera, which was still on the books right up to the reign of Pope John XXIII, whose benevolent charisms did not include physical agility. Bullfighting as condemned by Pius V was quite different from the present form, which was stylized only in the eighteenth century. The preponderant opinion of theologians is that the present form is morally licit, as the bullfighter's brains make him even with the bull's brawn. Just as the Council in Trullo stopped the clergy from going to horse races, the Fourth Lateran Council forbade clerics to engage in hawking and clamorous hunting (that would be riding with the hounds to the sound of brass horns), but this had nothing to do with the killing of animals. Pope Julius II was a keen hunter, and in more modern times, Pope Leo XII shot birds in the Vatican gardens for relaxation. The Council's strictures were really against wasteful consumption of time. Today the equivalent of hawking and hunting as languorous misuses of time by clerics obviously would be golf, whose appeal is irresistible to those with an inflexibility of mind.

There is a real moral doubt about professional boxing, no less today than in the days of bare knuckles and even John L. Sullivan's compromise with two-ounce gloves. This is based both on its deliberate intent to inflict serious injury and on the corruption of promoters, which has figured in the decline of its popularity. I tend to consider "professional sports" almost a contradiction in terms, anyway, and would no more pay to watch others play than I would pay to watch others eat. Two minutes of listening to commentators on one of the sports channels is sheer mental anesthesia. Because of physical danger in professional boxing, especially in the heavyweight class, it is only reasonable to require careful monitoring. There are more concussions, orthopedic injuries, and neurological damage in football than in boxing, and the life expectancy of an NFL player is less than that of a professional boxer. Remarkably, cheerleaders in the NFL reported four times more injuries than did the players. Amateur boxing, of which I sing, ranks seventy-first in sports injuries, far below even baseball and soccer.

In a fallen world, there always will be excesses, and in my book *Coincidentally*, I described Mike Tyson biting off the ear of Evander Holyfield. I now can add to that because, just one hour before I began to write this, I ran into a bartender walking along Park Avenue who had served a non-alcoholic drink to Tyson at the start of his career and prophetically called him "Champ". Gratuitous violence seems to be going mainstream with the rise of Mixed Martial Arts, which should be banned for its otiose incitement of bloodlust.

Holyfield's robe was inscribed with the text: "I can do all things through Christ who strengthens me" (cf. Phil 4:13). Little did he know that he was about to become another Malchus. Saint Paul may very well have been a boxer. He refers to the races and boxing in 1 Corinthians 9:24–27. The "corruptible crown" was a reference, not to the Olympian games of Athens, but to the Isthmian games of Corinth, which had been restored by Julius Caesar in 44 B.C. Long before the victor's wreath was of ivy, the Isthmian wreath had been of fast-wilting celery leaves. Pindar even mentioned it: "I sing the Isthmian victory with horses, not unrecognized, which Poseidon granted to Xenocrates, and sent him a garland of Dorian wild celery for his hair, to have himself crowned."

The Apostle to the Gentiles did not consider the Way of the Lord Jesus a spectator sport. "Well, I do not run aimlessly, I do not box as one beating the air; but I pommel my body and subdue it, lest after preaching to others I myself should be disqualified." No young man should venture into the larger world without having sparred with his peers, and boxing should be required of every seminarian who would preach like Paul. The writer to the Hebrews (12:4–13) quite likely took counsel from the apostle when he wrote:

In your struggle against sin you have not yet resisted to the point of shedding your blood. . . . The Lord disciplines him whom he loves. . . . God is treating you as sons; for what son is there whom his father does not discipline? If you are left without discipline, in which all have participated, then you are illegitimate children and not sons. . . . For the moment all discipline seems painful rather than pleasant; later it yields the peaceful fruit of righteousness to those who have been trained by it. Therefore lift up your drooping hands and strengthen your weak knees and make straight paths for your feet, so that what is lame may not be put out of joint but rather be healed.

28

MAKING MUSIC

L IKE PROUST'S "episode of the madeleine" that occasioned an involuntary flood of memory, I remembered a flush of things when I
chanced upon a Coolidge-Dawes campaign button among items in one
of my grandmother's souvenir boxes. Charles G. Dawes was a fitting
companion for the classically trained Coolidge, whose eloquence has
been ignored by jaded historians. Coolidge was the last president to
write his own speeches, and the so-called "Silent Cal" held an informal,
chatty press conference every week. Without teleprompters, he honed
his words and many of them were lapidary: "It is a great advantage
to a president and a major source of safety to the country for him to
know that he is not a great man."

Dawes, a successful businessman, was a son of Ohio and then Ne-
braska and became the only vice president to be awarded the Nobel
Peace Prize when it meant something. He was the architect of the
Dawes Plan for reparations after World War I. Eventually he became
ambassador to the Court of Saint James. But what involuntarily sprang
to mind when I saw that campaign button was music. Dawes had taught
himself to play the piano and was a composer. The only other public
figure around that time to compose was Mayor Jimmy Walker, who,
in 1910, had written the song "Will You Love Me in December as
You Do in May?" By almost every human measure, the mayor was
unlike the vice president, and he did not pretend to moral heights. I am
told that he dutifully attended Mass every Sunday in my old Church

Originally published in *Crisis Magazine*, September 6, 2012.

of Saint Agnes on East Forty-Third Street, reverently refraining from receiving Communion because of his irregular domestic arrangements. As a different sort of musician, Dawes was classical in taste and in 1912 composed for piano and violin his celebrated "Melody in A Major". In the very year he died, 1951, it was made into a popular song, "It's All in the Game", which outsold Jimmy Walker's vaudeville number.

The number of public officials who have actually composed music is small, although many have been musicians. Condoleezza Rice did us proud with her performance before the Queen in Buckingham Palace, but we still suffer the occasional politician playing aesthetically unsettling music on an acoustic guitar. Among heads of state, Harry Truman rose at five each morning to practice piano for two hours before going to school. When Paderewski visited Kansas City, he gave the sixteen-year-old Harry a private instruction in how to play his Minuet in G. As vice president, he was forbidden by Mrs. Truman to perform in public after he was photographed in an Army canteen playing on an upright piano with the actress Lauren Bacall sitting on top. He performed the Paderewski minuet for a group of Methodist ladies in 1945 and told them, "When I played this, Stalin signed the Potsdam Agreement." John Quincy Adams was a flutist, Woodrow Wilson treasured his violin, and Warren G. Harding could play every instrument in a band he organized except the slide trombone and E-flat cornet. The decline from Thomas Jefferson playing Vivaldi, Corelli, and Haydn on his Amati violin to William Jefferson Clinton playing "Heartbreak Hotel" on his saxophone with a vigor that outmatched his competence, is another hole in the balloon of social Darwinism. In recent times, King Frederick IX of Denmark's House of Glücksburg both played the piano and conducted orchestras. King Bhumibol of Thailand plays the clarinet. As heads of state in waiting, Crown Prince Naruhito plays the viola, and Prince Charles is a cellist.

Among heads of state who were composers as well as players, David soothed Saul with his harping and seems to have annotated the singing of the Psalms. There is the hapless case of Nero, who made the Romans listen to his compositions. Richard Coeur de Lion delighted in being his own minstrel. And there are Henry VIII, who may have written "Greensleeves", and George III, who only began to compose for the harpsichord after he went insane. Then there was the edgy King Ludwig II of Bavaria, patron of Wagner, who endowed the Staatstheater am Gärtnerplatz in Munich. Farther back were the especially fecund Thibault IV of Navarre and Alfonso X of Castile; and Louis XIII of France, whose motets and a ballet are extraordinary. The Hapsburgs are in a category of their own, because all of them from Frederick II to Karl VI were composers. Frederick the Great wrote 121 flute sonatas and a symphony plus some marches. Though not a head of state, Albert of Saxe-Coburg and Gotha, eventually Prince Consort in 1857, played the organ to the delight of Mendelssohn in 1842 and composed more than forty published works, mostly lieder, some of which are still performed. Richard Nixon is said to have composed for violin and piano, both of which he played. When Jósef Piłsudski was president of the Second Republic of the land that gave us Chopin, it is not surprising that his prime minister was Ignacy Paderewski. As an aside, one notes that George III's consort, Queen Charlotte, the mother of fifteen children, chose as her music master Johann Sebastian Bach's eleventh son, Christian, and sang an aria in 1764 to the accompaniment of an eight-year-old Mozart. Considering that Mozart was the last of seven children, J. S. Bach the last of eight and the father of twenty, and the tenor Johann Haydn, a younger brother of Joseph, whose father's seventeenth child was born when he was sixty-three, artificial contraception would have greatly reduced the world's repertoire of music.

Back to my original theme, Vice President Dawe's "Melody in A Major" enchanted Fritz Kreisler, who made it one of his signature pieces. As a prodigy, Kreisler had entered the Vienna Conservatory at the age of seven, and then, with the support of his Jewish father, who worked hard to pay his expenses, he studied in Paris under Bruckner, Hellmesberger, and Massenet and came to the United States in 1888 to perform in Steinway Hall at the age of thirteen. At one point, in a state of dejection after failing to be admitted to the Vienna Philarmonic because of his vibrato, Fritz gave up the violin to study medicine, but he returned, and in 1910, the Catholic master Sir Edward Elgar dedicated to him the "Violin Concerto in B Minor", which Kreisler had commissioned and performed at its premiere. Later on, Kreisler lived in New York City at 2 Sutton Place, where Bishop Fulton Sheen, then an auxiliary bishop, met him while calling on a neighbor. Soon he received Kreisler into the Church. The great musician had a great soul and studied the Scriptures diligently in Hebrew and Greek. He adapted one of his compositions to a waltz tune as theme music for Sheen's television program. Shortly before his death, he became blind and deaf in a traffic accident, but he was uncomplaining and died with edifying serenity in 1962. Kreisler was probably the last major performer to use catgut for strings. Possibly with Kreisler in mind, Sheen frequently used the image of beautiful music coming from the gut of a cat, but in this he was mistaken, since catgut usually is from sheep's intestines. But that is better than the fourth string on Paganini's violin, which was said to have been an intestine of his mistress, whom he had murdered, although Liszt denied this.

It does seem that an ear for music goes along with a gift for languages, and Kreisler was a polyglot. Sheen was virtually tone deaf, and although his French was grammatical and fluent, he spoke it with a poor accent. Kreisler took an interest in the building of the Church of Our Saviour of which I was the sixth pastor. Bishop Sheen often remarked that he was to be the first pastor but that did not work out for reasons known best to him and Cardinal Spellman. He lived across the street and often visited what are now my rooms. I think the good bishop would be pleased to see in my study a fine bust of Kreisler, carved in 1949 by the Czech sculptor Mario Korbel. It came my way by almost miraculous circumstance. Carved on it are the opening notes of his "Liebesfreud".

These were some of the memories that infused themselves when I came across that Coolidge-Dawes campaign button, and, if they ramble a little here and there, they are, after all, involuntary. It is just that some of this might be worth noting, or else it could be lost. I should give the last word to John Henry Newman, whose sister, Harriet, thought that he had the potential to become another Paganini, although we assume not in every detail. Newman took up the violin at the age of ten and performed for his Oxford colleagues, for the near destitute children of Littlemore, in his Oratory school, and alone, even composing for a comic opera. He writes in *The Idea of a University*: "Music, I suppose . . . has an object of its own . . . it is the expression of ideas greater and more profound than any in the visible world, ideas, which centre indeed in Him whom Catholicism manifests, who is the seat of all beauty, order, and perfection whatever, still ideas after all which are not those on which Revelation directly and principally fixes our gaze."

29

POPE BENEDICT'S DECISION

W HAT GOD KNOWS is not necessarily what God wills. Each pope is guaranteed the protection of the Holy Spirit from fallible definitions of faith and morals, but to suppose that each pope is there because God wants him there, including the unworthy successors of Peter, comes close to the unforgivable blasphemy against the third Person of the Holy Trinity. Twenty-year-old Benedict IX was at least as nightmarish as his successor, Gregory VI, who usually is counted with his predecessor among the popes who relinquished their office. There are times, though, when the hand of God is not manhandled, and that, for instance, is why Cardinal Cooke once told me that he had never been so conscious of the presence of the Holy Spirit as he was in the conclave that elected John Paul II. It may also be that the sudden death of John Paul I, as stunning as recent events in the Vatican, was not untimely if it was part of a higher plan.

The Petrine office is not indelible like Holy Orders, and, in 1415, Gregory XII nobly and efficiently made his resignation a kind of security for healing the Western Schism. Dante was so frustrated by what he considered dereliction of duty that he put the abdicated Celestine V into the Inferno, but that was his own *Commedia*, when the Church, not in fancy but in fact, recognized the fact that he is in heaven. In 2009, photographs were widely circulated showing Benedict XVI leaving his pallium at Celestine's tomb, and many commentators then thought that this was more than a gesture of incidental piety.

Originally published in *Crisis Magazine*, February 13, 2013.

As with the Spiritual Franciscans as a whole, almost in tandem with the earlier Montanists, Celestine V proved the utter impracticality of dovelike innocence without serpentine astuteness, and Boniface VIII was as right as was John XXII in condemning these "Fraticelli". But Boniface also proved the desperate shortcoming of cleverness without innocence. Benedict XVI's serene retreat to pray will not be like the last months of Pope Celestine, who might nearly qualify as a martyr for the terrible treatment he endured for ten months until death when immured in the walls of the Fumone castle about forty-three miles southeast of Rome. Celestine was confined to an unsanitary cell hardly large enough for a bed and an altar. We see in this the contempt that venal souls have for the motives of the humble, and Celestine was nothing if not humble. The role of Boniface in Celestine's degradation has often been sanitized, but, as John Henry Newman wrote in the *Historical Sketches*: "Glosses are put upon memorable acts, because they are thought not edifying, whereas of all scandals such omissions, such glosses, are the greatest." A decree of Boniface, making hay of the misfortunes of his saintly predecessor, spelled out for the first time the canonical case for papal renunciation:

> Pope Celestine V, Our predecessor, whilst still presiding over the government of the aforesaid Church, wishing to cut off all the matter for hesitation on the subject, having deliberated with his brethren, the Cardinals of the Roman Church, of whom We were one, with the concordant counsel and assent of Us and of them all, by Apostolic authority established and decreed, that the Roman Pontiff may freely resign. We, therefore, lest it should happen that in course of time this enactment should fall into oblivion, and the aforesaid doubt should revive the discussion, have placed it among other constitutions *ad perpetuam rei memoriam* by the advice of our brethren.

Benedict XVI certainly has known all this, for perhaps not since the Lambertini pope Benedict XIV has there been a pope of such mental acuity and historical erudition, nor probably has any pope since Gregory I, in his writings and witness, matched the magisterial eloquence and liturgical sensibility of this pope of Bavaria. The verdict of centuries from now will affirm the spiritual electricity of his Regensburg lecture and how he spoke to the French academics in 2010 and, if words be immortal, his undying words in Westminster Hall.

His general audiences regularly outnumbered those of his beloved pre-decessor, and those accustomed to spectacle actually began to listen to the crystalline reasoning of what he said. Before he became pope, any form critic could detect his hand in Vatican documents when turgid prose suddenly broke into clarity. His first-rate mind did not indulge the tendency of lesser minds to obscure what is profound and to think that what is obscure is perforce profound.

If he was expected to be a caretaker pope, he took care very well, proving himself unexpectedly radical in his reform of reform, which is more difficult than reform itself, for it restores the form that reformers forgot. So we had the renewal of liturgical integrity in an ecology of beauty, streamlining of the Curia, greater attention to episcopal ap-pointments, the overdue beatification of Newman with all its portents for theological science, the Anglican Ordinariate, which may be less significant for what it becomes than for the fact that it exists at all, and progress with the Eastern churches. His plans, like all "the best laid schemes of mice and men", were not completely realized. Not all that Benedict called "filth" was removed, and we can be sure that a media eager to affect being scandalized will point out among those entering the conclave those who bring with them the shadows of what Benedict tried to dispel. But he continues to dignify in charity even those who may not understand that "dignitas". He announced his renunciation of office in Latin and by so doing indicated his hope that even if some of those listening may have mingled astonishment with incomprehen-sion, his successor would be able to speak the official language of the Church he leads and the city he governs.

According to the postulator for the Cause of John Paul II, as early as 1989 Wojtyła had signed a letter of renunciation to be invoked should he become incapacitated. He reaffirmed this in 1994, but in the same year he told the surgeon operating on his broken leg: "I have to heal. Because there is no place in the Church for a Pope Emeritus." It is only human to be so conflicted, and John Paul II opted against renun-ciation. The fact that Pope Benedict had scheduled various journeys, canonizations, and an encyclical to be published "within the first six months of 2013" would indicate that his decision to step down, if con-sidered a possibility for a while, was made more suddenly. As Prefect of the Congregation for the Doctrine of the Faith, he must have suffered patiently when he saw decisions made that he would not have wanted made. And had he become pope sooner, many tragedies, such as the Legionaries of Christ scandal and other defacements of the Church, would have be handled far differently. Although he is younger than Leo XIII, who slogged on until his ninety-third year, and his physical condition is far better than that of his predecessor in his last years, the experience of those years had to have shaped his present decision.

In an age of dangerously limited attention spans and fickle loyalties, there is a danger in proposing that popes last only as long as people want them. Romans have long said with their typical insouciance that when one pope dies, you just make another one: "Morto un papa se ne fa un altro." As everyone dies, it was important that John Paul defied the aimless Culture of Death by showing how to die, but that witness also came at the cost of care of the churches. There were times then when the Church Militant seemed in freefall, and the man who then was Cardinal Ratzinger must have anguished much in silence. He did not, however, trim the truth as he knew it and went so far as to say that a certain passage in *Gaudium et Spes* of which young Wojtyła was a principal architect was "downright Pelagian". Cardinal Dulles observed: "The contrast between Pope Benedict and his predecessor is striking. John Paul II was a social ethicist, anxious to involve the Church in shaping a world order of peace, justice, and fraternal love. Among the documents of Vatican II, John Paul's favorite was surely the pastoral constitution *Gaudium et Spes*. Benedict XVI, who looks upon *Gaudium et Spes* as the weakest of the four constitutions, shows a clear preference for the other three."

The personality cults of our present age had to a degree shaped the young in the Church who had known only one pope. A most attractive charism of Benedict XVI has been his desire to vanish so that the faithful might see only Christ: "cupio dissolvi". He strengthened the papacy by vaulting sanctity over celebrity. In a grand paradox, nothing in him has become so conspicuous as his desire to disappear. Christ gave the Keys to a Galilean fisherman with a limited life span. He chose Peter; Peter did not choose him. When the pope relinquishes the Petrine authority, he does not submit a letter of resignation to any individual, for the only one capable of receiving it is Christ. This is why "renunciation" or "abdication" is a more accurate term than "resignation" in the case of the supreme pontiff. Unless this is understood, the danger is that a superficial world will try to refashion the pope into some hind of amiable but transient officeholder. Popes are not Dutch royalty. On the other hand, Queen Elizabeth II has one tiara, not three, but the longer she wears it, the more she seems to grow in the affection of her people, which bond of respect is morally more powerful than any constitutional grant of rights and privileges. But the papacy's authority is absolute and not gratuitous, and its exercise cannot be only conditional and validated by human approval. Pope Benedict pays tribute to that imperial obligation of his office by willing to relinquish it.

To risk the sort of truism that gets to be what it is by being true: Nothing is permanent in this world. The world is older than our centuries and cannot stop changing. We speak of papal protocols in the Middle Ages as if they happened long ago, but only from our limited perspective were they in the middle of anything. In view of recently found evidence that the declining dinosaurs may finally have been wiped out by an asteroid 66.03 million years ago, the Middle Ages might as well have been when my alarm went off this morning. Study of the amino acids in the eyes of bowhead whales now reveals that these magnificent creatures can live over two hundred years, and there may be a whale in the Arctic right now that swam those same waters during the War of 1812. Line up ten of those whales, and you are at the Resurrection. From that perspective, we should speak cautiously about Rome as the Eternal City. "Sub specie aeternitatis", Rome really was built in a day. Pope Benedict attests by word and example: that "Here we have no lasting city, but we seek the city which is to come" (Heb 13:14).

30

GLORIOUS JANITOR

T HE JANITORS, doormen, and apartment superintendents in my parish and I have a particular fraternal bond, for we are situated to
observe the private lives of many. They are called upon at inconve-
nient hours to do tasks and handle emergencies uncongenial to those
in some other lines of work. The term "janitor" is related to the Roman god Janus, who guarded doorways, protecting the goings in and
out of people as well as of years themselves and transitions in one's life,
which is how we get the month January. Ovid and Cicero were of the
opinion that the name Januarius was derived from the Latin verb "ire",
meaning "to go", which makes sense, with relation to doors and years.
The Vatican Museum has a statue of Janus Bifrons, so called because
he has two faces, and that is an advantage if you have to keep an eye, or
eyes, out for people. The pagan god is only on display in the Vatican
for aesthetic and anthropological reasons, and no one lights candles
before it, but the name was not uncommon among Christians, and so
we have the patron martyr of Naples whose blood liquefies.

It would also seem that janitorial service is a good school of sanctity:
it has produced, among others, Saint Martin de Porres and Saint André
Bessette and the Venerable Solanus Casey. After all, "I had rather be
a doorkeeper in the house of my God, than to dwell in the tents of
wickedness" (Ps 84:10). That is the King James translation, while the
Douay-Rheims renders "janitor" as "abject", indicating that janitors
did not enjoy much prestige among some translators. But both are better than the absurdity that appears in the New Jerusalem Bible: "Have

Originally published in *Crisis Magazine*, November 14, 2012.

you met the janitors of Shadowland?" (Job 3:8–17). It paints a picture of people pushing brooms in an amusement park.

As for Janus, to be called two-faced if you are not a god is not a compliment. When called two-faced by a political opponent, Abraham Lincoln asked, "If I had two faces, would I be wearing this one?" Joseph Dutton was a janitor and anything but two-faced in the weak sense. With the recent canonization of Marianne Cope, his name has cropped up obliquely. It may be that he is a saint above and could qualify for official recognition as such someday here below.

He was given the name Ira when he was born on April 27, 1843, to Methodist parents in Stowe, Vermont. It was the same day that another native Vermonter, the Mormon founder Joseph Smith, married his scribe William Clayton in Nauvoo, Illinois, to a second wife, Clayton's own sister-in-law. His family moved to Janesville, Wisconsin, four years later, where his life was one of conventional piety. As a teenager he worked in a library and taught in Sunday school. Caught up in the excitement of recruiting bands at the start of the Civil War, he enlisted in the Thirteenth Wisconsin Infantry, showing business prowess as a quartermaster as well as nursing the wounded and burying the dead. After the war, he stayed on as a volunteer, tracing the remains of missing soldiers and later, in the War Department, settling the claims of survivors. When he was discharged in 1866 as a captain, only a paucity of commissions deterred the temptation to make a career in the army, and for the next twenty years he took on various kinds of work, including jobs in an Alabama distillery and a railroad in Tennessee.

He had impetuously married a woman he met in the war. Later on, he called the marriage "one of those things I have tried to forget". Failing to reform her unstable habits, which brought him to the brink of bankruptcy, and enduring her infidelities about which he had been warned, he finally filed for divorce in 1881 long after she had left him for another man. Disconsolate over the failed marriage and haunted by memories of the war, he became a severe alcoholic and spent ten years in a "drunken stupor" often collapsed in gutters. This was a time, he said, of "sinful capers". But he was able to time his drinking for the evenings so that he still worked with discipline. "I never injured anyone but myself." This, he admitted, was a kind of two-faced Janus existence, which one day in 1876 he vowed to quit, and he never drank from that time on. And as Janus was the god of transitions, he made a spiritual change, too: the influence of Catholic friends brought him to study the faith, and on his fortieth birthday he was received into the Church, changing his name to Joseph.

A desire to do penance for the rest of life drew him to the Gethsemani Trappist monastery in New Haven, Kentucky, which had been founded in 1848 and was still small and rather unstable in governance. He always remained grateful for the twenty months he spent there, remembering the monastery in his will and from then on calling himself "Brother Joseph", although he never took religious vows. In his process of discernment, he decided that he was called to a penitential but active life.

The work of Father Damien de Veuster among the lepers of Molokai was already well known, and, without any notice, he sailed from San Francisco to Hawaii in the summer of 1886. Transferring to a boatload of lepers, he arrived at Molokai, to the surprise and consternation of Father Damien, who told him that he could not afford to pay him anything. Brother Joseph expected no pay and supported himself until he died in 1931. His days were spent as a janitor, cleaning the primitive shelters, scrubbing floors, while also building latrines and outbuildings and bandaging sores, as well as helping Mother Marianne Cope in keeping records and organizing arriving patients. Like Mother Marianne and unlike Father Damien, he never contracted Hansen's Disease. When Theodore Roosevelt had the ships of the Great White Fleet salute the grave of Father Damien as they sailed by, Brother Joseph waved a large American flag from shore. Always the patriot, even at the age of seventy-four he tried to enlist in the army at the outbreak of the First World War, trying on his old Civil War sword belt before he was turned down.

In 1889, Father Damien said, "I can die now. Brother Joseph will take care of my orphans." As he grew older, Brother Joseph was said to become more radiant in spirit, and when he was eighty-three, he confessed: "I am ashamed to think that I am inclined to be jolly. Often we think we don't know that our Lord ever laughed, and here my laugh is ready to burst out any minute."

There actually was widespread interest in Brother Joseph in his later years, and he received letters, including one from President Harding in 1923, lauding his work. But he never left Molokai, and he is buried next to the man now known as Saint Damien. The glorious janitor wrote, "It seems a mere accident that I ever heard of this place, and it might never have happened again." Of course it was not an accident at all.

31

MOTHER CHURCH AND THE NANNY STATE

THAT THE FILM about the Cristero Rebellion, *For Greater Glory*, has been news to many highlights the appalling ignorance of history in our culture. That isolation from the human experience has made it easy to confuse conscience with emotion and think religion is irrational. George Neumayr has written, "In one of his memoirs, Obama uses the Old Testament story of Abraham and Isaac to argue that secularism equals 'reason' and religion equals 'crazy caprice'."

Such was the distillation of President Obama's commencement speech at Notre Dame University, in which he said, "It is beyond our capacity as human beings to know with certainty what God has planned for us or what He asks of us." Fast forward, and the same university has joined a legal action against the consequences of the presidential speechwriter's half-baked Kantianism.

If Fidel Castro is the unwitting founder of modern Miami, so Barack Obama may be remembered for unintentionally energizing the Catholic bishops. He may even have brought some of Europe to a more sober frame of mind about his policies. The throngs in European cities welcoming the advent of Hope and Change during his campaign were unsettling enough for anyone who remembers the cheering crowds gathered in some of those same platzes in the 1930s. In short order, the Nobel Peace Prize became the Nobel Promise Prize when it was awarded to someone who was expected to do great things even if he had not done so already. *L'Osservatore Romano* was pleased that the

Originally published in *Crisis Magazine*, June 22, 2012.

new president might bring an end to Reagan's "neocon revolution" and hailed this election as "a choice which unites".

Hired editors are not anointed prophets, but this became painfully obvious a year later when the foreign affairs editor of *L'Osservatore*, Giuseppe Fiorentino, said that Obama's position on abortion and other life issues had not confirmed fears of radical change. Around the same time, the editor-in-chief of *L'Osservatore*, Gian Maria Vian, defended Obama's speech at Notre Dame and added: "We have noticed that [Obama's] entire program prior to his election was more radical than it is revealing itself to be now that he is president. So this is what I meant when I said he didn't sound like a pro-abortion president."

During the mass starvation in Ukraine in 1933, Walter Duranty informed readers of the *New York Times* that "there is no famine or actual starvation nor is there likely to be any." Duranty received the Pulitzer Prize, which so far, at least, has been denied to Baghdad Bob. It does seem that editors of various journals object to the proposition that facts should take precedence over theory. Even one United States bishop hailed the Obama election as "a great step for humanity". But that was before reality raised its head. Some bishops projected their own virtue onto civil figures and then were shocked that a president would lie to them, rather like Neville Chamberlain, incredulous that the Germans were insincere in their protocols and ungentlemanly in starting a war on a weekend.

Until the Calles Law of 1926 "for Reforming the Penal Code" restricted the Church in Mexico, the hierarchy had hoped for some kind of accommodation. Pope Pius XI announced to the world, without apparent success, that the Cristeros persecutions were like those of the Roman Emperor Decius. Still, the heroic witness of the Mexican bishops was not monolithic in strategy. Bishop Francisco Orozco y Jiménez of Guadalajara was so outspoken that he had to go into exile three times, as far as Chicago. Saint Athanasius only had to repair to the desert. There was also the problem of opportunists exploiting a good cause for selfish motives.

As opposition to the HHS mandate now may tempt some politicians to join the fray, for personal stratagems, even if they do not share the moral issues at stake, so in 1928 some anticlerical Freemasons joined the Cristeros simply because they were on the outs with the Calles and Portes Gil governments.

In December of 1926, the bishops of the United States wrote a pastoral letter in support of the suffering Church in Mexico, written in a clear and Catholic diction that could have been a useful template for our time:

> A written constitution is an instrument which enumerates and defines the rights and duties of government, distributes its powers, prescribes the manner of their exercise, and limits them to the end that the liberties of the citizens may be preserved. Since the purpose of government is to protect human rights, not to destroy them, it follows that the charter by which a government operates cannot contain a grant of unlimited power. For the exercise of such power would be tyranny, inasmuch as it would tend to destroy rights which both the natural and the positive laws of God place beyond the jurisdiction of men. Hence, in the commonly accepted American doctrine, a constitution vests the government with such rights and powers as are necessary for the proper exercise of its just functions, and at the same time forbids it to encroach upon rights of a higher order which come to men, not from the people, nor from the State, nor from any aggregation of States, but from the Creator of both men and States, almighty God. This conception is wholly in keeping with the teaching of the Catholic Church.

Then they cited the 1888 encyclical of Pope Leo XIII, *Libertas praestantissimus*:

> (Liberty of conscience) may also be taken to mean that every man in the State may follow the will of God, and, from a consciousness of duty and free from every obstacle, obey His commands. This, indeed, is true liberty, a liberty worthy of the sons of God, which nobly maintains the dignity of man, and is stronger than all violence or wrong —a liberty which the Church has always desired and held most dear. This is the kind of liberty the apostles claimed for themselves with intrepid constancy, which the apologists of Christianity confirmed by their writings, and which the martyrs in vast numbers consecrated by their blood.

An almost instinctive reflex in modern times to mortgage Mother Church to the Nanny State makes it hard in an entitlement culture to teach old bureaucrats new tricks. Recent "talking points" issued by a group hostile to the bishops' opposition to government mandates stress that in the past two years the federal government has given $1.5 billion to Catholic charitable organizations. Certainly, this funding may promote the general good, but he who pays the piper still calls the tune, and the tune has now become raucous. If it is hard to reform the instincts of church bureaucracies, nothing is impossible with God. That is one of the things we know with certainty about God, contrary to the theosophy of an honorary Doctor of Laws from Notre Dame University.

The bishops of the United States have called for daily prayer leading up to the fourth of July to safeguard freedom of religion in our country. The new style of the federal government, in speech after speech, to replace freedom of religion with freedom of worship is not innocent of calculation, for while permitting ritual acts of devotion within the walls of a building, it would limit the right to express religious beliefs in public discourse. In Orwellian semantics, soon enough even the commandment to love the sinner but hate the sin becomes "hate speech". There are some religions, like some governments, that are intrinsically hostile to freedom of religion. Recently, a Christian in Tunisia was martyred for converting from Islam, and his killers chanted prayers against "polytheists", as they call Christians, while slowly slicing off his head. While this happens frequently, our own federal government and much of the media are conspicuously silent, for while they may not be interested in religious creeds, they demur from what the Second Vatican Council's "Declaration on Religious Freedom" called "immunity from coercion in civil society". By way of antidote, Ronald Reagan said in his first gubernatorial inauguration speech in 1967, "Freedom is a fragile thing and is never more than one generation away from extinction."

The great crises of cultures are crises of saints. This is hard to understand if you think religion is a substitute for clear thinking. In a review of *For Greater Glory*, a scandalized Roger Ebert spoke of the film's "Catholic tunnel vision":

> One important subplot involves a 12-year-old boy choosing to die for his faith. Of course the federal troops who shot him were monsters, but the film seems to approve of his decision and includes him approvingly in a long list of Cristeros who have achieved sainthood or beatification after their deaths in the war.

If, as Obama says, "It is beyond our capacity as human beings to know with certainty what God has planned for us or what He asks of us", then any witness to the faith will be at the very least in bad taste and at worst in madness. Preferable would be those "useful idiots" whom Lenin played as puppets.

Not yet listed in the ranks of martyrs is the former ambassador to Wales, or rather Malta, Douglas Kmiec, who said, "(Obama) is inclined to the view of the First Amendment that the government is not intended to be hostile to religion. It is intended to be accommodating when it can."

Or Nancy Pelosi who does her religion "on Sundays and not at a press conference". Or Kathleen Sebelius, who thinks "we have a lot of reeducation to do." And Vice President Biden, who as a confessor of the faith said, "The next Republican that tells me I'm not religious I'm going to shove my rosary beads down his throat."

Of a different temperament was Saint Justin Martyr, whose testimony before the Roman prefect under the emperor Marcus Aurelius is meticulous in its details:

> The prefect Rusticus said: "Now let us come to the point at issue, which is necessary and urgent. Gather round then and with one accord offer sacrifice to the gods." Justin said: "No one who is right thinking stoops from true worship to false worship." The prefect Rusticus said: "If you do not do as you are commanded you will be tortured without mercy." Justin said: "We hope to suffer torment for the sake of our Lord Jesus Christ, and so be saved. For this will bring us salvation and confidence as we stand before the more terrible and universal judgment-seat of our Lord and Savior." In the same way the other martyrs also said: "Do what you will. We are Christians; we do not offer sacrifice to idols."
>
> The prefect Rusticus pronounced sentence, saying: "Let those who have refused to sacrifice to the gods and to obey the command of the emperor be scourged and led away to suffer capital punishment according to the ruling of the laws." Glorifying God, the holy martyrs went out to the accustomed place. They were beheaded, and so fulfilled their witness of martyrdom in confessing their faith in their Savior.

The Fortnight of Freedom starts on the vigil of the feast of Saints John Fisher and Thomas More. As the latter summed it up, they knew the difference between their sovereign and their Savior.

32

I AM NOT MAD

H AVING SPENT more than a few years dealing with mental patients, nine of them as a chaplain to a large state mental hospital, I thought I was pretty well informed about the etiology of psychosis. When I had to deal with a distressed individual whose symptoms were unlike any I had ever encountered, I asked a close friend, who is one of our nation's most distinguished psychiatrists, if there is a term for such a psychosis, and he replied that, based on the information I had given him, the best definition is "nut".

That must have been more or less what the Roman governor Porcius Festus thought of Saint Paul. The apostle had been imprisoned for two years, in conditions inferior to those of most modern penitentiaries, by Felix, the predecessor of Festus, for causing social unrest. The problem was that Paul's alleged crimes had to do with religion, and the Romans did not want to get involved in matters concerning Judaism or anything outside the purview of the civil legal system. As the Greeks were nothing if not philosophers, so the Romans were paramount lawyers, and, at their best, they had no equals. Saint Paul knew that, and he also had heroic humility, which dispenses with modesty, so that he knew and could boast that he was a good lawyer himself and could play the astringent Romans like a piano, including the "most excellent Festus".

When the King of Galilee, Julius Marcus Agrippa II, came to the coastal city of Caesarea with his sister, Julia Bernice of Cilicia, with whom he was said to have had an incestuous relationship, Festus told

Originally published in *Crisis Magazine*, June 13, 2012.

them with Roman hauteur about this Paul of Tarsus, who spoke of "one Jesus, who was dead, but whom Paul asserted to be alive" (Acts 25:19). Here we have a very modern scene: public figures living louche lives, and bored enough to welcome the diversion of an "interesting" legal case. Mix with that a nervousness about taking religion too seriously and a kind of detachment about "a certain Jesus". I suppose that the avenues of any contemporary city are filled with people who pass by churches and think that they have something to do with "a certain Jesus". But they quickly pass by because that remote figure was said to have been alive after he died. A lovely thought, but those who take it seriously are certifiable candidates for public mental institutions. Festus abandoned the understatement of noble Roman tribunes and shouted, "Paul, you are mad; your great learning is turning you mad!" He assumed that Paul was the sort of fanciful intellectual the sober Romans disdained, living in a fantastic ivory tower while the sturdy Romans built real towers and sturdy aqueducts and solid bridges, and so he became irrational in the face of reason. Paul answered calmly, "I am not mad, most excellent Festus, but I am speaking the sober truth." Agrippa then added to the chorus by saying half sardonically, "In a short time you think to make me a Christian." One thinks here of the wife of Pontius Pilate, who, albeit perhaps superstitious, had suffered much because of Jesus in a dream.

Addressing the "most excellent Festus" with the serene self-control that has truth and reason on its side, the bishops of the United States are standing up against bullying by our present government. This discomforts those vague Catholics who prefer Caesar and his seductive largess to Christ and his atoning sacrifice. It must especially frustrate the naïve socialists who thought that "social justice" was their copyrighted mantra, only to see groups of orthodox believers demonstrating for religious freedom outside government buildings.

I recently received a note saying that the bishops of our nation are exaggerating the state of things and that the people who follow them have "drunk the Kool Aid". I should be glad to challenge that complainer in public debate, but the note was anonymous, as one expects when there is no substance to such a view beyond pique. It took me a while to learn that people who are mad can make a cogent case for their sanity. But all heaven and the best of human civilization since the first Christian century attest that Paul was not crazy, and on the

Feast of the Holy Trinity, we celebrate the mystery that must puzzle those who define reality on their own terms and even seems madness to those whose prejudices are the only measure of sanity. Saint Paul, having outwitted the miniature sophisticates in the amphitheatre of Caesarea, let the greatest of all mysteries and the source of all joy slip from tongue to pen when he ended a letter announcing the identity of God: "The grace of the Lord Jesus Christ and the love of God and the fellowship of the Holy Spirit be with you all" (2 Cor 13:14).

33

THE FATHER OF OUR COUNTRY

T HE ECLECTIC national Presidents' Day homogenizes our veneration of the man General "Light-horse Harry" Lee eulogized as "first in war, first in peace, and first in the hearts of his countrymen". It also neglects Abraham Lincoln, who with the Father of our country made a pair unmatched for virtue and genius appropriate to their tasks in the annals of any nation.

Both had cause to treat with Catholics, who, in Washington's time, were an exotic minority and who were only beginning their ascendancy in the years of Lincoln. In the frigid trials of Valley Forge, Washington had to explain to many of the ignorant among his troops that the Guy Fawkes celebrations were unworthy of the cause of the nascent nation. He banned the distraction on November 5, 1775, by an Order in Quarters:

> As the Commander in Chief has been apprized of a design form'd for the observance of that ridiculous and childish custom of burning the Effigy of the pope—He cannot help expressing his surprise that there should be Officers and Soldiers in this army so void of common sense, as not to see the impropriety of such a step at this Juncture; at a Time when we are solliciting, and have really obtain'd, the friendship and alliance of the people of Canada, whom we ought to consider as Brethren embarked in the same Cause. The defence of the general Liberty of America: At such a juncture, and in such Circumstances, to be insulting their Religion, is so monstrous, as not to be suffered

Originally published in *Crisis Magazine*, February 20, 2012.

or excused; indeed instead of offering the most remote insult, it is our duty to address public thanks to these our Brethren, as to them we are so much indebted for every late happy Success over the common Enemy in Canada.

General Washington was pragmatic, of course, and not inspired by any theology higher than the sort instinctive to a gentleman who knows that he is a creature accountable to a Creator. Relations with British North America, that is, Canada, had their twists and turns. The following year, John Carroll, who would become the first Catholic bishop in the new United States of America, went to Quebec on behalf of the Continental Congress along with his cousin, Charles Carroll, Catholic signatory of the Declaration of Independence and a chief financer of the revolution, accompanied by Samuel "Old Bacon Face" Chase and Benjamin Franklin in an unsuccessful attempt to start a rebellion by French Canadian Catholics. It was a task entirely out of order for a man in Holy Orders, and the Bishop of Quebec, Jean-Olivier Briand, promptly excommunicated him. In 1784, the Propagation of the Faith, working through the Nuncio to Versailles and Benjamin Franklin as the United State's minister to Louis XVI, began to design a structure for the Catholic Church in the new nation. "For the first time only, and by a special grace", Pope Pius VI allowed the priests of the United States to elect their bishop, and twenty-four of the twenty-six electors chose Carroll in 1789, and he was consecrated the following year in England. It would be anachronistic to call Carroll an Americanist, in the sense of the term used by Pope Leo XIII, but he had some opinions not unaligned with that disposition. Carroll wanted local election of bishops to become a regular custom and delicately refused to publish Rome's condemnations of Freemasonry, his own brother Daniel being a Mason as well as a Catholic. As for the liturgy, he wrote in a letter of 1787:

> Can there be anything more preposterous than an unknown tongue; and in this country either for want of books or inability to read, the great part of our congregations must be utterly ignorant of the meaning and sense of the publick office of the Church. It may have been prudent, for aught I know, to impose a compliance in this matter with the insulting and reproachful demands of the first reformers; but to continue the practice of the Latin liturgy in the present state of things

must be owing either to chimerical fears of innovation or to indolence and inattention in the first pastors of the national Churches in not joining to solicit or indeed ordain this necessary alteration.

Bishop Carroll and General Washington were sympathetic in their common notions of deportment. Carroll had been trained by Jesuits in French Flanders, and, at the age of sixteen, Washington copied out "110 Rules of Civility & Decent Behavior in Company and Conversation", which are often attributed to him, although they are based on the book of manners published by the Society of Jesus. Carroll kept a slave, whom he freed in his will with a substantial monetary bequeathal. During his episcopate, the Jesuits in Maryland owned some four hundred slaves. As for abolition, Carroll, with an eye to William Wilberforce, proposed:

> Since the great stir raised in England about Slavery, my Brethren being anxious to suppress censure, which some are always glad to affix to the priesthood, have begun some years ago, and are gradually proceeding to emancipate the old population on their estates. To proceed at once to make it a general measure, would not be either humanity toward the Individuals, nor doing justice to the trust, under which the estates have been transmitted and received.

In the next great national crisis, Lincoln appeared to save what Washington had founded. For Lincoln, the model and mold of the presidency was Washington himself, though Lincoln's religious attitudes were more fungible, attaining a convincing ardor in his last years. Washington's Masonry was of the eclectic, if not syncretistic, sort typical of men with natures healthier and sentiments more temperate than the menacing anticlericalists of Europe. He freely attended Catholic Mass during the Continental Congress and, upon becoming president, penned his famous letter to John and Charles Carroll, in which he said:

> As mankind become more liberal, they will be more apt to allow, that all those, who conduct themselves as worthy members of the community, are equally entitled to the protection of civil government. I hope ever to see America among the foremost nations in examples of justice and liberality. And I presume that your fellow-citizens will not forget the patriotic part, which you took in the accomplishment of their revolution and the establishment of their government, or the

important assistance, which they received from a nation in which the Roman Catholic faith is professed.

I thank you, Gentlemen, for your kind concern for me. While my life and my health shall continue, in whatever situation I may be, it shall be my constant endeavour to justify the favorable sentiments you are pleased to express of my conduct. And may the members of your society in America, animated alone by the pure spirit of Christianity, and still conducting themselves as the faithful subjects of our free government, enjoy every temporal and spiritual felicity.

In 1895, Pope Leo XIII addressed the bishops of the United States in his encyclical *Longinqua oceani*:

Nor, perchance did the fact which We now recall take place without some design of divine Providence. Precisely at the epoch when the American colonies, having, with Catholic aid, achieved liberty and independence, coalesced into a constitutional Republic the ecclesiastical hierarchy was happily established amongst you; and at the very time when the popular suffrage placed the great Washington at the helm of the Republic, the first bishop was set by apostolic authority over the American Church. The well-known friendship and familiar intercourse which subsisted between these two men seems to be an evidence that the United States ought to be conjoined in concord and amity with the Catholic Church. And not without cause; for without morality the State cannot endure a truth which that illustrious citizen of yours, whom We have just mentioned, with a keenness of insight worthy of his genius and statesmanship perceived and proclaimed. But the best and strongest support of morality is religion. She, by her very nature, guards and defends all the principles on which duties are founded, and setting before us the motives most powerful to influence us, commands us to live virtuously and forbids us to transgress.

That was about a century after the Father of our country was buried at Mount Vernon, ten years before Leo was born. But a contemporary of Washington, when told by the Pennsylvania-born painter Benjamin West that the General intended to lay down the powers of his office and return to his farm, said, "If he does that, he will be the greatest man in the world." The speaker, popularly known as "Farmer George" himself, was King George III.

34

NEWMAN AND THE ANGLICAN PATRIMONY

O N MY SIXTIETH BIRTHDAY, friends gave me a spiritual bouquet, and, as there are a variety of spirits, they included a bottle of 1945 Armagnac. When I open that bottle, I shall be able to smell the liberation of Paris, but the question is: When should I open such a valuable thing? James Anthony Froude recalled that "though (Newman) rarely drank wine, he was trusted to choose the vintages for the college cellar." While good souls have been sipping the wine of Newman all these years like sommeliers arguing over the taste, it is now time to drink it full. For when Pope Benedict beatifies the great man, *Deo volente*, this year, he will be telling the world that the vintage pressed long ago is full ready for general consumption. Newman has been remaindered too often to the pantheon of beloved intellects whose poetic charm overcame the distractions of their religion, the same way temperamentally fragile revisionists played down Francis of Assisi as a mystical stigmatist and turned him into an ecological birdbath ornament.

Newman was born in his day for today. The Established Church of his youth, which seemed like a flagship of empire, is now breaking on the shoals of reality, and what Newman proposed as a challenge to something mighty is now a call to rescue survivors. Yet in any such calamity there are both flotsam and jetsam. Pope Benedict's decision on November 4 of 2009 to receive Anglicans in a canonical personal ordinariate was a response to an appeal. He is not rummaging for flotsam, those floating logs who will drift to any safe shore. The pope welcomes

The Portsmouth Institute Conference, Portsmouth Abbey, Rhode Island, June 11, 2010.

a full profession of faith in the Catholic creeds and a rejection of all that the sectaries have said in their contradiction. The jetsam are those who have been propelled by circumstance into a positive recognition that their old craft was not the Barque of Peter. In the opening paragraph of the apostolic constitution *Anglicanorum coetibus*, the Holy Father says, "The Apostolic See has responded favorably to such petitions. Indeed, the successor of Peter, mandated by the Lord Jesus to guarantee the unity of the episcopate and to preside over and safeguard the universal communion of all the Churches, could not fail to make available the means necessary to bring this holy desire to realization."

I may stand accused of mixing metaphors of wines and ships, but sailors have never thought the two incompatible. If it is time to break open the wine of Newman, it is not like drinking the last dregs on a sinking ship, for it is very like uncorking a noble vintage that has been waiting for a special celebration. What Newman preached in his "Parting of Friends" at the time of his conversion, and what he wrote heart to heart in his *Apologia* and summed up in his "Biglietto Speech", have all found their moment now.

It is important to remember that Newman was classically trained. It is difficult for us to recreate a semblance of what that means in our coarsened culture, whose leaders are so bereft of those articles of civility and wisdom which were the common language of types diverse as Cicero and Lord Chesterton and Harry Truman. Newman's classical acuteness enabled him to tell the real thing from a sham. The logician Richard Whately said he had never known such a clear thinker. The Established Church of his youth was a mixture of spiritual aridity and institutional confidence, well expressed by Mr. Thwackum in Henry Fielding's *Tom Jones*, who says: "When I mention Religion, I mean the Christian Religion; and not only the Christian Religion, but the Protestant Religion; and not only the Protestant Religion, but the Church of *England*." We can go back earlier. One of the most splendid, if also most obtuse, lines ever uttered about churchmanship was that of the seventeenth-century Anglican Bishop of Ely, Simon Patrick, who praised "that virtuous mediocrity which our church observes between the meretricious gaudiness of the Church of Rome and the squalid sluttery of fanatic conventicles". Newman, though, knew that classical mediocrity is not what fuzzy thinkers today think it to mean when they address the religious controversies of our time in the turgid diction

of Delphic oracles. Horace praised the man who loved well the Golden
Mean, "Auream quisquis mediocritatem diligit." It was golden, not because it was a compromise between truth and falsehood, but because it
was like a laser beam pointing the way between every mistake. Anglicanism, by force of political circumstance and religious confusion, had
settled on a wrong idea of the Golden Mean as a "via media" of a bit of
this and a bit of that, reducing the apophatic spirituality of Byzantium
to polite ambiguity. Newman gave a series of lectures between 1830
and 1841 in defense of Anglicanism's via media as spiritually prudent
and the work of divine grace, but the scandal of the Jerusalem bishopric
in 1841, which laid aside religious differences between Anglicans and
Lutherans for the sake of practicality, would open Newman's eyes to
the fact that the true "via media" is a declaration of precision and not
vagueness. So he says, "Take England, with many high virtues, and
yet a low Catholicism. It seems to me that John Bull is a spirit neither
of heaven nor hell. . . . Has not the Christian Church, in its parts, sur-
rendered itself to one or other of these simulations of the truth? . . .
How are we to avoid Scylla and Charybdis and go straight on to the
very image of Christ?"

This subjective substitute for the classical Golden Mean is not modern but postmodern, since the philosophical quality of our culture
has tumbled from those parapets upon which wrong but well-trained
thinkers could declare that the only certitude is that nothing is certain.
Today, what Pope Benedict has tagged "the dictatorship of relativism"
is seen in a blithe rejection of Christian essentials by vestigial Anglicanism, not because they are hard to believe but because they were never
learned. So let us uncork the wine of Newman, for what he preached
while still an Anglican has now found its target:

> Surely, there is at this day a confederacy of evil, marshalling its hosts
> from all parts of the world, organizing itself, taking its measures, en-
> closing the Church of Christ as in a net, and preparing the way for a
> general Apostasy from it. Whether this very Apostasy is to give birth
> to Antichrist, or whether he is still to be delayed, as he has already
> been delayed so long, we cannot know; but at any rate this Apostasy,
> and all its tokens and instruments, are of the Evil One, and savour
> of death. Far be it from any of us to be of those simple ones who
> are taken in that snare which is circling around us! Far be it from us
> to be seduced with the fair promises in which Satan is sure to hide

his poison! Do you think he is so unskilful in his craft, as to ask you openly and plainly to join him in his warfare against the Truth? No; he offers you baits to tempt you. He promises you civil liberty; he promises you equality; he promises you trade and wealth; he promises you a remission of taxes; he promises you reform. This is the way in which he conceals from you the kind of work to which he is putting you; he tempts you to rail against your rulers and superiors; he does so himself, and induces you to imitate him; or he promises you illumination, —he offers you knowledge, science, philosophy, enlargement of mind. He scoffs at times gone by; he scoffs at every institution which reveres them. He prompts you what to say, and then listens to you, and praises you, and encourages you. He bids you mount aloft. He shows you how to become as gods. Then he laughs and jokes with you, and gets intimate with you; he takes your hand, and gets his fingers between yours, and grasps them, and then you are his.

Pope Benedict XVI has done a stunning thing in providing such an ecclesial structure as described in the Apostolic Constitution *Anglicanorum coetibus*. The dilemma of Anglicans maintaining a firm if incomplete belief in the supernatural character of the apostolic Church, when contradicted by postmodern forces who would reduce the creedal formulas to impressions of reality, is a cultural icon of the spiritual combat between virtue and egoism that defines the crisis of our age. While only the pope knows what he is doing, I suspect that this constitution is a shot fired over the bow of secular cynicism that is entwining its fingers with those of the men and women of our generation to make us one with the enemy of our Creator.

Consider the fact that many Catholics have reduced sacred worship to a suburban expression of goodwill. It is evidence of the creeping banality by which the Prince of Lies would seduce Holy Church herself, though he is bound to fail, with that same mediocrity which repulsed Newman, for he knew that banality is indeed evil and possibly crueler than pre-Christian paganism, which danced its sensuality in Arcadian groves without feeling a post-Christian need to declare perversity a sacrament.

As late as 1835, ten years before his conversion, Newman associated the Antichrist with the papacy and returned from his first visit to Rome in 1833 calling Catholicism "polytheistic, degrading, and idolatrous". Gradual experience of alternatives to Catholicism, however, especially the skepticism of the Broad Church Anglicanism of his coterie, trimmed his judgment: "We are much disposed to question whether any tests can . . . prove that the Roman communion is the Synagogue of Satan." His friendly battles in Oxford with his mentor, Richard Whately, whom I have mentioned, professor of political economy (battles that he said continued when he was starting the Catholic University in Dublin, where Whately had become Anglican Archbishop), moved him to reflect more on the Catholic claims. Whately was a fair-minded man who advocated civil rights for Catholics and Jews. He had his own sense of humor, which inspired him to satirize the new skeptical biblical critics by using their critical methods to prove that Napoleon Bonaparte never existed. In this, he was a precursor of Ronald Knox, who, a century later, used modern canons of literary criticism to prove that Tennyson's poem "In Memoriam" had in fact been written by Queen Victoria. In treating virtue ethics and the Greek ideal of happiness as "eudaimonia", it was Dr. Whately who said, "Happiness is no laughing matter." Newman inherited something of this subtlety, and this should help to make sense of what Newman meant later when he said, "as a Protestant, I felt my religion dreary but not my life—but, as a Catholic, my life dreary, not my religion." Understanding true happiness as the attainment of truth, he was ready to sacrifice lesser consolations to find it, like Augustine exulting in the discovery of "beauty ever ancient, ever new". The recent proposal of a personal ordinariate for Anglicans is an invitation to such "eudaimonia".

Newman preached big words to a small scene in his day. He was addressing a "national apostasy" that is now universal. If "national apostasy" seemed an inflated term when Keble decried the government's confusion of bishops with state managers, Newman did not see it so, and he called it the start of the Oxford Movement. The Oxford Movement has now become a World Movement, sometimes called a "Reform of the Reform", the kind of *aggiornamento* optimistically envisioned but imprecisely achieved in the years after Vatican II. *Anglicanorum coetibus* may well be the ecumenical movement come of age, a correction of the disoriented notion that unity in the Church happens by confederation. While the number of ecclesial communities that will join this new structure for Anglicans may be small, the initiative itself could encourage relations with the separated historic Churches.

More than thirty years ago, John Paul II approved a "Pastoral Provision" to receive Anglicans into the Catholic Church. This followed the 1976 decision of the General Convention of the Episcopal Church to ordain women. Some five years before that, I had written my first, and perforce juvenile, book, which was a small study of this question. In it, I maintained that to deny gender as a charism in the sacrament of orders was a Gnostic heresy, for it dismissed the prophetic significance of sexuality. In phrases subtle because I knew the subject would be scandalous, I contended that such ordinations would irreparably destroy chances for unity with the Catholic Church and that this Gnostic abuse of anthropology would logically lead to what is now called same-sex marriage. Some reviewers said that was absurd. What I predicted in 1971 has happened. There have been many divisions since then within the Anglican structure that prided itself on its unity, even in this country through the trials of the Civil War. The original Pastoral Provision provided welcome for over one hundred clergy and several thousand laity, including one religious community of women. These are small numbers, but they have established several flourishing parishes with an approved Anglican Use for worship that is attractive even to cradle Catholics. While the most important aspect of this provision was the clear signal of Rome indicating that the question of women's ordination belongs to the irreformable deposit of sacred tradition, the part of it that got most attention was permission for the ordination of married men, with the understanding that, as in the Eastern rites, there could be no marriage or remarriage, in the instance of widowhood, after ordination.

It seems logical that this provision, while continuing as an entity, would be subsumed by the new personal ordinariates. The chief difference between the former pastoral provision and the new ordinariates is precisely that, while the former was part of the regular diocesan structure, the new ordinariates would have their own bishops and ecclesiastical superiors similar to military ordinariates. This is something that Newman, with all his prophetic gifts, could not have anticipated. While he encouraged a scheme of Ambrose Phillipps de Lisle for a sort of Anglican Uniate Church for converts, he knew that it was impractical. Yet, his comment in a letter to de Lisle in 1876 is significant: "Nothing will rejoice me more than to find that the Holy See considers it safe and promising to sanction some such plan as the Pamphlet suggests. I give my best prayers, such as they are, that some means of drawing to us so many good people, who are now shivering at our gates, may be discovered." It is also the case that in his day the invalidity of Anglican orders was not a settled question as it is today. Newman was ordained a priest in 1847, less than two years after he had been received into the Church, and Manning's ordination in 1851 took only nine weeks, and within fourteen years he became Archbishop of Westminster. That was during the pontificate of Pius IX, who was not given to impetuosity or neglect of doctrine.

The new apostolic constitution expectedly has had its doubters. The Holy Father made this a personal initiative, to the surprise of some ecumenicists whose more relaxed instincts had not encouraged traditionalist Anglicans in their petitions. I do not make an exact parallel with the present situation, but in a letter of 1859 to Lord Acton, Newman wrote: "There will necessarily always be round the pope second-rate people, who are not subjects of that supernatural guidance which is his prerogative." Newman was certain that the Catholic Church in England could not flourish if she remained under the jurisdiction of the Propaganda Fidei, but he was often stymied in getting his message through bureaucratic tangles to the pope. He said, "the Rock of St. Peter on its summit enjoys a pure and serene atmosphere, but there is a great deal of Roman *malaria* at the foot of it."

The uniqueness of *Anglicanorum coetibus* naturally begs questions. Not least of these is the "patrimony" of Anglicanism that the apostolic constitution seeks to safeguard, not temporarily but as a permanent ornament of the richness of the Latin Church. But this patrimony is not defined. Anglicanism has gone through transformations since the Elizabethan Settlement, and the engine of its motion, which is now proving to be not perpetual, has been its effort to define itself in various moods, Catholic, Calvinist, Laudian, Erastian, Deist, Evangelical, Tractarian, Ritualist, Liberal, and Post-Christian, all bobbing on the surface of the endemic Anglo-Saxon bias of Pelagianism. The "patrimony", however reimagined from time to time, would have been more Protestant from the start were it not for the theological conservatism of Elizabeth I. Surely there were clerics, especially of the Laudian period, who were "stupores mundi" in their Patristic erudition, but often what claimed to be a return to sources was a sort of theological bottom-feeding made palatable by a knowledge of Greek. To speak in generalities of a patrimony risks becoming nostalgic, bearing in mind that nostalgia is history after a few drinks. John Jewell and Richard Hooker in the sixteenth century had a romantic notion of the subapostolic church that easily accommodated what their queen decreed. Even Jewell had a functional but not sacramental concept of episcopacy, and his confidence was in Sola Scriptura. Anglicanism was not originally confessional but statist, and what is of the state dies with the neglect of the state. As Caesar's eye grows cold, so does what glimmered in his glance.

As far as aesthetic patrimony goes, the typical Anglican forms of worship are no more elevated than the ordinary Catholic liturgy of our day, now happily under revision. Newman was sensitive to signs; he remembered wearing black gloves in Trinity College Chapel when mourning the daughter of King George IV, the Princess Charlotte; and everyone knew he had abandoned Anglican orders when he appeared one day in grey trousers. If he who blushed at the most innocent pun had seen some of the liturgical aberrations of our generation, he would have lapsed into a coma. There is a cottage industry of polemicists who claim that the Catholic Newman used to haunt old Anglican churches to hear the voices of distant choirs gilding the rafters. There is no evidence for that. His frequent discouragements were not from a loss of what he had sternly rejected. He writes of those who claimed that the convert keeps looking back over his shoulder: "This is said of every one in turn—and in every case which I am acquainted with most falsely —There is but one feeling of joy and happiness among those persons with whom I am acquainted who have become Catholics."

Newman was actually repulsed by much of what passed for prayer in the churches of his early years and said that the thought of the Anglican service made him "shiver". The services in his own university church of Saint Mary in Oxford were "intensely dreary". The Tractarians spent little time on the liturgical romanticism of the ritual movement that was to follow. But that movement was a recovery of a patrimony not unique to the English church. Perhaps in recognition of this, it has been suggested that the new personal ordinariates should revive the Sarum Rite to be distinct. In my Anglican days, I knew no one who had ever seen the Sarum Rite. That would just be a homemade historicism, which in part is why a proposed revival of the Sarum Rite for the new Westminster Cathedral was rejected in the nineteenth century. The personal ordinariates will fail if their concept of preserving a cultural patrimony is the creation of an Anglo-Saxon Theme Park or an ecclesiastical Williamsburg. It would lack the spiritual dynamic the Church needs for revitalizing a dispirited segment of our anemic culture. Pope Benedict's focus has always been on Newman rather than on Anglicanism, but in the foreword to a book *Turning Towards the Lord*, by the Oratorian priest Father Lang, he commended the *ad orientem* position of the celebrant at the altar and described "the contribution made by the Church of England to this question and in giving, also, due consideration to the part played by the Oxford Movement in the nineteenth century". Many of the present Anglican clergy were not reared in the Anglican tradition themselves, and this adds a difficulty if the "patrimony" that the Constitution seeks to encourage is in no small part an "ethos" that comes by a long lived experience of a cultural heritage.

There follows another question about the expectations of Anglican stalwarts who waited so long to become Catholic, since all veneer of Catholic simulation was shattered by the ordination of women more than thirty years ago. Catholicism is a commitment and not a last resort. Pusey was discomfited when Newman continued to attract converts after his conversion. After an awkward encounter in Prior Park in Oxford, Newman wrote to his friend Dalgairns saying that Pusey had expected the Catholic converts to be nothing more than vinedressers who had simply "transferred to another part of the vineyard". Newman became aware, and expresses this in multiple ways in his lectures on "Certain Difficulties Felt by Anglicans", that High Anglicanism is a delusional ecclesiology supported by cultural affinities holding sway over logic. Newman dispatches this with curt words in the *Apologia* when he says, "It is not at all easy (humanly speaking) to wind up an Englishman to a dogmatic level."

The Prefect of the Congregation for the Doctrine of the Faith, Cardinal Levada, said on March 9, 2010 that "among the distinctive elements of Anglican heritage should be included the spiritual and intellectual gifts of the Oxford Movement in the nineteenth century. The then-Anglican cleric Newman, together with his fellow Tractarians, have left a legacy that still enriches a common Catholic patrimony." Thus the Anglican patrimony consists in a style of living the apostolic life. Newman and his fellows gave it new life by opting for the fullness of Catholicism, in an action rooted in an intuition of history ignored in our own day. Newman's argument for the development of doctrine as an economy requiring what he called "preservation of type" and "chronic vigor" is the antecedent cousin of Pope Benedict's

"Hermeneutic of Continuity". The Holy Father might paraphrase with benevolent Bavarian courtesy what Newman said rather curtly: "To be deep in history is to cease to be a Protestant."

After attending one of Newman's twelve lectures on "Certain Difficulties Felt by Anglicans" delivered in London in 1850, which provide a guide for wavering Anglicans today, Thackeray rose from his seat, daunted by the Newmanian logic, and cried out: "It is either Rome or Babylon, and for me it is Babylon." The case is the same today, to a larger audience: It is either Rome or Babylon. These lectures, treated nervously by some who would tone down Newman's popery, are the beating heart of the exhilarated Catholic Newman. It is noteworthy, but not inexplicable, that perhaps the leading modern Anglican interpreter of Newman, Owen Chadwick, in his book *The Spirit of the Oxford Movement* (1990), does not once refer to the lectures on "Certain Difficulties Felt by Anglicans". In them, Newman said, "All depends on the fact of the supremacy of Rome", and "One vessel alone can ride those waves; it is the boat of Peter, the ark of God."

In 1988 I made the longest of all possible trips on this planet, the treacherous and usually fruitless journey from Oxford to Cambridge. I went to hear a lecture by Cardinal Ratzinger. To the dismay of some of the faculty who attributed the vast outpouring of undergraduates to what one professor called the current young people's fad for mediaevalism, Ratzinger spoke of eternal verities in a way that I imagined might have been composed by Newman. Both are musicians— Newman a violinist, and Ratzinger a pianist. And you see that I speak of Newman in the present, because he is being brought back to us by Ratzinger, whose own name will never be in the past perfect. The pope's overture to Anglicans is not polemical but pastoral. Newman said, "Denunciation neither effects subjection in thought nor in conduct." In the new apostolic constitution, the Holy Father denounces no one, but as the Father of Christian Unity, in the succession of Peter, who was commanded by Christ to confirm the brethren in the faith, he would that none be lost.

In this conference you will hear talks more serviceable than mine, I am only here as the sommelier, to recommend the vintage wine of Newman. He uncorked it in the finale of the *Apologia pro Vita Sua* when he listed his friends who had joined him in the fraternity of converts and also those who were moved in mind but not enough in will to embrace the ancient beauty. He wrote one last line: "And I earnestly pray for this whole company, with a hope against hope, that all of us, who once were so united, and so happy in our union, may even now be brought at length, by the Power of the Divine Will, into One Fold and under One Shepherd."

35

THE CATHOLIC BUCKLEY

THE DEFINITION OF the Catholic Church as "Here comes everybody" is one of those quotations said to have been said by someone who did not say it. James Joyce has the line in *Finnegan's Wake*, but it is not clear if Joyce meant it for the Church. We do know that when he left the Catholic Church, a lady asked him if he had become a Protestant, and Joyce replied to the invasion of his privacy: "I've lost my faith, not my reason." So Joyce indicated that if he was an atheist, he was at least a Catholic atheist. William Buckley was a Catholic theist, and anyone who even obliquely encountered his circle of friends, which seemed to include almost everybody, found that circle a bit like Pascal's circle, whose center is everywhere and whose circumference nowhere. Bill would have delighted in saying that Pascal cribbed that definition from Nicholas of Cusa, who cribbed it in turn from Empedocles, and that Voltaire typically claimed it as his own. The Buckley circle of friends would have included all of them, and if Bill was the center, its circumference included all who are here had they met him.

John Henry Newman was an inspiration to our subject, and not more appropriately than now when I say that in his circle Bill was Newman's prototypical gentleman, who "makes light of favours while he does them, and seems to be receiving when he is conferring" and who does not slander or gossip, treats his enemy as a potential friend, and is "merciful towards the absurd". His mercy was even extravagant, as when he told a "Firing Line" guest: "I would like to take you seriously, but to do so would affront your intelligence." That quality of

Originally published in *Crisis Magazine*, May 19, 2014.

mercy was strained once, as I recall, in an exchange at the Democratic Convention in Chicago, and then he produced a long and elegant article explaining himself. I think, in that instance, he sensed that he was dealing with an individual whose dark views were not of this world.

A postmodern relativist finds it hard to believe that someone really does believe. If someone professes Christianity, he assumes that there must be another motive. For the postmodernist is essentially a watered-down Kantian, that is: a narcissist without the moral imperative. Such a person analyzes others primarily in terms of how they helped or neglected him. This is typical of our "Me Generation", but it has antecedents all the way back to Eden. One example is the lugubrious Baron von Hügel, who decided that Newman was not a saint because he did not express joy. Now, a wiser man pointed out that the only recorded instances of Newman not seeming joyful were the three times he was visited by von Hügel. One can be so focused on the self that one is oblivious to the effect one has on others. This is a subtle and untutored sociopathology that can have results that are not mild. It certainly makes for bad biography.

Self-referential cultural dilettantes will not understand what Christopher Dawson meant: that there can be no culture without worship of something other than the self. They will think that Buckley's worship of God was one of his little ways, a harmless culturism or romantic eccentricity in an otherwise worldly man. They will try to perpetuate his political philosophy without his reverential memory. But that definition of Buckley, with religion as one vestigial element among many other components, is nothing more than the pedantic Gradgrind's approved description of a horse as quadruped, graminivorous, and so on. Buckley as a political commentator and writer who attended Mass on Sunday is not Buckley at all. His race for mayor of New York showed that he was more Cincinnatus than politician, and he even sniffed something déclassé in politics for its own sake and considered the term "professional politician" a louche oxymoron.

Buckley knew that piety is a virtuous combination of reverence for God and one's ancestors, and by making man ageless it saves him from the conceit that thinks that his generation is the first in history to have come of age. Some of his finest writing was the special art forms of obituary, eulogy, and panegyric. This he did with a special skill for members of his own family, which is the most difficult craft. His "autobiography of faith" is dedicated to his mother. His richest inheritance from his father was his religion. It is highly significant that he always added "Jr." to his name, long after his fame eclipsed his father's, for it was from his father that he learned the faith of his fathers. It is also important that in a society in which marriage has become a temporary convenience instead of a sacrament, he was a faithful husband for fifty-seven years in sickness and in health until death. Without that covenantal understanding of human obligations, the philosophy of conservation is doomed to dwindle into an aesthetic sentiment.

When Buckley died, the *Chicago Tribune* was one of many such journals that called him a "national institution". I suppose that being a national institution is better than being in one, but that kind of rhetorical embalming cannot dismiss the man so easily. There are things more portentous than national institutions, and any nation unaware of that eventually ceases being a nation at all. This is why Whittaker Chambers served as a kind of Saint Paul to Buckley. Chambers knew that the struggle against Communism was one battle in a spiritual warfare vaster than nations and as old as original sin. "For we are not contending against flesh and blood, but against the principalities, against the powers, against the world rulers of this present darkness, against the spiritual hosts of wickedness in the heavenly places" (Eph 6:12). If you want a description of the Catholic Buckley, it will be not like Gradgrind's horse but like Chamber's witness, for Chambers wrote: "A witness, in the sense that I am using the word, is a man whose life and faith are so completely one that when the challenge comes to step out and testify for his faith, he does so, disregarding all risks, accepting all consequences."

Buckley spelled Catholicism with a C both majuscule and minuscule. His humane fraternity included all who were humane. He eulogized his friend Richard Clurman saying that he had "always subconsciously looked out for the total Christian, and when I found him, he turned out to be a non-practicing Jew. It will require the balance of my own lifetime to requite what he gave to me." By so saying, he echoed the Biglietto Speech of Newman, who admired in the classical liberalism of his day that "which is good and true; . . . the precepts of justice, truthfulness, sobriety, self-command, benevolence". That tribute, however, was not left as a dangling sentiment of indifferentism. Newman disdained a vague philanthropy that holds that there is no positive truth in religion, but that one creed is as good as another. . . . It is inconsistent with any recognition of any religion, as true. It teaches that all are to be tolerated, for all are matters of opinion. . . . Since, then, religion is so personal a peculiarity and so private a possession, we must of necessity ignore it in the intercourse of man with man. If a man puts on a new religion every morning, what is that to you? It is as impertinent to think about a man's religion as about his sources of income or his management of his family. Religion is in no sense the bond of society.

In his collected speeches (*Let Us Talk of Many Things*), Buckley quotes Bernard Iddings Bell: for many, religion now seems "an innocuous pastime, preferred by a few to golf or canasta". One evidence of the depth of Buckley's eschatology was his neglect of golf. He had nothing against it, nor did I ever hear him mock people who collect butterflies or watch professional sports, but I do not think he could explain why so many homo sapiens do those things.

He was persuaded by the Catholic interpretation of man and so convinced that, while he had many difficulties about doctrine, as he tried to thrash them out most energetically if eclectically in his book *Nearer, My God*, he said in good conscience that never once had he ever questioned his faith. This is exactly what Newman explained by saying that "a thousand difficulties do not make one doubt."

Buckley's approach to theology was not an apologia but an inquiry, which is why he called his book *Nearer, My God* and explained: "That is an incomplete phrase, but then my thoughts are incomplete, and I pray that my faith will always be whole." He should have been pleased that a reviewer of it in *The National Catholic Reporter*, which he found useful as a source of wrong opinions on almost every subject, said "Read it and wince, read it and weep, read it and smile, but read it." His maieutic approach to theological conversation could be a difficult labor, rambling and tentative. As he put it, "Truth is a demure lady, much too ladylike to knock you on your head and drag you to her cave. She is there, but people must want her and seek her out." He struggled to understand the systematic analysis of Paul VI's *Humanae Vitae*, but he lived long enough to know that it was perhaps the definitive prophecy of the modern age, and all the demographic, moral, and political denouements of these subsequent decades prove that its warnings and predictions, which contemporaries mocked as histrionic, were in lamentable fact understated. His final response was the logic of the Logos: "The answer, for a Catholic, has got to be: the position taken by the Pope, as spokesman for the magisterium."

High moments in the annals of the *Firing Line* included discussions about the soul with Mother Teresa and Malcolm Muggeridge. Lesser in that order was a program on Liberation Theology, the hot theological topic of the day, in 1984. He and I and the late moral theologian Monsignor William Smith made it seem like discussing economic dialectic at the Congress of Vienna. A transcript of that program is available on Amazon with a current sale ranking of 5,477,441. But Bill said it had the most voluminous viewer response of any program up to that date. I do remember receiving a letter from a woman who thought the Swiss government was planning concentration camps in Paraguay.

He was chronically annoyed by the canard that he had authored the cynical prescription "Mater Si, Magistra No" in reference to the quip that appeared in one line of the *National Review*'s gossip column. He regretted that its flippancy lent itself to abuse and wrote to a Jesuit publication: "Do [the editors of *America*] sincerely believe that I have decided to reject the depositum fidei because along came an encyclical whose rhetorical emphases disappointed me? Proceed, if you like, publicly to despair over our insouciance or frivolity but to edge us into infidelity is more than uncharitable; it is irrational, and in the true sense, scandalous."

Buckley was not a clone of Waugh's Rex Mottram, who thought that the pope could predict the weather. He was on solid ground in distinguishing magisterial pronouncements and prudential prescriptions and in his fear that truths may be expressed by John XXIII's *Mater et Magistra* in ways that could be coopted "by such declared enemies of the spiritual order as the New Statesman and the Manchester Guardian, which hailed the conversion of the Pope to Socialism!" Here was an affinity with some of the "inopportunists" of the nineteenth century, who accepted the dogma of papal infallibility while questioning its timing. Later, his profound reservations about Paul VI's *Populorum Progressio* and more serious criticisms of a weaker document on economics by the bishops of the United States were vindicated by John Paul II's *Centesimus Annus*. One wishes he were with us as Benedict XVI prepares his next encyclical on a similar subject. Buckley enjoyed whimsically posing as the other side of the papal coin, infallible in matters not having to do with faith and morals. And nothing fascinated him more about the papacy, and nudged him into the realm of holy humility, than the fact that when he and David Niven were presented in a private audience, John Paul II had not the slightest idea who they were.

His favorite prayer was the Rosary, the busy man's Oratory, and he often used his fingers instead of the beads, especially on airplanes. I know he often prayed the Rosary for others. He was as ordered in his religious practices as in the discipline of his writing, and they were part of a whole, since man's work is a means of sanctification if done well for a high purpose. He died at his desk, which, dare I say, had become a prayer desk. Of course, modern liturgical revisions were a mortification, and he told of a wedding in the hyperactive Novus Ordo use that he attended with Pat, whom he wryly called an "innocent Anglican". She clutched his hand and asked what was going on. He hesitatingly tried to defend the happy-clappy rituals: "My own reaction had been the protective reaction of the son whose father, a closet drunk, is spotted outside his household unsteady on his feet." Blessedly, he lived to see the first stages of Pope Benedict's "reform of the reform". Given his affinity for words, he did not suffer lightly the gingerly misuse of English infinitives in the vernacular translation, and he felt a personal wound when the American bishops approved the absurd infelicities in a neutered translation of the Bible.

On his eightieth birthday, I suggested that he was a good age for the papacy, though we knew that his marital state and speaking engagements precluded that. Nonetheless, I proposed as his papal motto Psalm 44:2: "Lingua mea calamus scribae, velociter scribentis" (My tongue is the pen of a writer writing fast.) That might have tempted him. He was also serious about Lent. When he sent me one of his Blackford Oakes novels, I wrote to him saying that, even from my remote perspective, his description of the protagonist's act of carnal congress was gratuitous and anthropologically unconvincing. He replied that we should discuss this, if I were permitted to do so during the penitential season. His Christian longing for death when death was due could only be thought suicidal for those who do not take eternity seriously and have never prayed for the grace of a holy death. He was very precise in consulting a priest about ordinary and extraordinary means of preserving life when Pat was dying, and he prayed for his own good death but in God's good time. He did not take counsel that excused sin.

Buckley's Fifth Gospel was human history itself, as it bore witness to the truth of the prophets. When he stood athwart history shouting "Stop!", he was yelling at human pride and not at the Lord of History. Catholicism describes history in big dimensions: Saint Augustine said that the Holy Gospel is deep enough for elephants to swim in and shallow enough for lambs to wade in. The Catholic vision, transcending tribalism and clannishness, is universal in a way more organic than international. Buckley was a Catholic before he was a conservative, and that saved his conservatism from both narrowness and nostalgia. Catholicism conserves a tradition of life itself, of which the Church is the embodiment, and anything less is philosophically tentative. For if the virtuous man is the totality of what man can achieve by nature, it is not the totality of what man is called to be by grace. "If we say we have no sin, we deceive ourselves, and the truth is not in us" (1 Jn 1:8).

Those words were written by the youngest apostle, John, who had watched Christ being crucified. In my own panegyric to Bill, I recalled a retreat, in this very abbey, when he led the recitation of the Stations of the Cross. I do remember his lengthy pause at the Ninth Station and his voice reading, "Jesus falls a third time." He said "third" differently from the way he said "first" and then "second". A third time. We imitate Christ because in his perfect humanity he imitated us who fall and fall and fall again. But Christ got up a third time, and so do we. That night Bill announced it was time for confession, and he led me into this abbey church. As I recall, we both tripped into a thorn bush, having already been attacked by some vicious sand flies. When we could not find a light switch, he said, "I can get around this church in the dark." I have since read into that a metaphor more than he meant. I do know that he regularly made his confession as a man who was not deceived. A man of natural virtue will ask forgiveness of other men, but a man of grace asks forgiveness of God.

Buckley was bemused by, but always convinced of, Hilaire Belloc's arch Catholic pronouncement in 1920 that "a man who does not accept the [Catholic] faith writes himself down as suburban." Buckley's manifold ways of saying this were a harpsichord transposition of Belloc's kettle drum, but the tune was the same, and it was not incidental music because the consequences of deafness to it were sinister and catastrophic. One day Bill telephoned me for the exact wording of lines Belloc had written after gazing upon the ruins of Timgad in North

Africa, a city destroyed by the Vandals after it had lost its cultural balance. I was happy that I could recall them and was moved that he had them rattling in his head. These are the words: "We sit by and watch the Barbarian, we tolerate him; in the long stretches of peace we are not afraid. We are tickled by his irreverence, his comic inversion of our old certitudes and our fixed creeds refreshes us; we laugh. But as we laugh we are watched by large and awful faces from beyond: and on these faces there is no smile." No smile. No smile on those faces behind the faces of the smiling biologist who assures us that a moral choice is justified by the autonomous act of choosing, and the smiling politician who promises change in the social order without regard for what is order, and the smiling jurist who says that "at the heart of liberty is the right to define one's own concept of existence, of meaning, of the universe, and of the mystery of human life." In contrast is that heir to a long classical culture, Benjamin Cordozo. Some contend that he was not the first Latino member of the Supreme Court, but he did graduate from Columbia University with honors in Latin. He knew the difference between sentiment and truth and said: "Opinion has a significance proportioned to the sources that sustain it."

I have said that Buckley was a Newmanian gentleman, but not a mere deontologized lightweight for whom conservatism is a thing that can survive without the classical tradition of culture. Buckley was well aware of the social vandal who has manners but no morals. Newman described the fatuous substitute for the real gentleman. Until recently, that sort was called a Yuppie, but now that specimen has spread into multiple types produced by the general neglect of the liberal arts and sacramental grace. In his *Idea of a University*, Newman describes these social characters common to various political schools today, who are incapable of mounting a political movement the way Buckley did because they are stagnant and cannot move themselves: "Mistaking animal spirits for vigour, and overconfident in their health, ignorant what they can bear and how to manage themselves . . . they have no principles laid down within them as a foundation for the intellect to build upon; they have no discriminating convictions, and no grasp of consequences. . . . They are merely dazzled by phenomena, instead of perceiving things as they are."

Political conservatism torn from the Theos that authored all life and the Logos that explains that life and the Beatific Vision that is life's ultimate promise will fade to a utilitarian calculus that, like its political opposite, finds the definition of life above its pay grade, thinks liberty is the grant of the government, and does not know what happiness to pursue. Without a higher vision to animate it, the secular conservative's City Set on a Hill will have little to distinguish it from the secular liberal's Upper West Side of New York. By a remarkable providence, the twelve-year-old Bill Buckley was at the Heston Aerodrome when Chamberlain waved the signed paper promising peace for our time. Bill would see many such barterings as the field changed from Fascism to Communism, but in each instance his belief in God recognized, in the spirit of accommodation with evil, the deadly sin of sloth, which is worse than naïveté.

In the short time since Bill's memorial Mass in the Cathedral of Saint Patrick, the two priests who flanked me at the altar, Father Fitzpatrick and Father Neuhaus, have died. Bill frequently discussed his faith with them in this life, but there are no disputations in the larger life where there are no maisonettes yet many mansions and no debates for all is song. One of my last dinners with Bill was joined by his nephew Michael, the Benedictine whose monastic life Bill said must be the happiest of all. We met in a private room at the New York Yacht Club —an unlikely place to discuss a Gospel that Christ preached from a small fishing boat in Galilee. I took it as an example of the development of doctrine. At the end of *Nearer, My God* he quotes Dom Michael's reminder that "agonia" is the Greek for "combat" and that a life that is not a daily spiritual combat is pitiful, for such a life is without love. Bill had not meticulously arranged his own last liturgy, and so I chose as one of the hymns a paraphrase of John Milton that we had sung together shortly before in my church:

He who would valiant be 'gainst all disaster,
Let him in constancy follow the Master.
There's no discouragement shall make him once relent
His first avowed intent to be a pilgrim.

Who so beset him round with dismal stories
Do but themselves confound—his strength the more is.
No foes shall stay his might; though he with giants fight,
He will make good his right to be a pilgrim.

Since, Lord, Thou dost defend us with Thy Spirit,
We know we at the end, shall life inherit.
Then fancies flee away! I'll fear not what men say,
I'll labor night and day to be a pilgrim.

36

VERBIEST: THE PRIEST WHO
INVENTED THE AUTOMOBILE

E VEN ONE WHO IS as maladroit as I when it comes to the internet profits from "YouTube", with its cavalcade of some of the great people and events of more than a century. Would that it could go back farther, but there are many moving scenes to which we have access. One shows Father Georges Lemaître, father of the "Big Bang" with Albert Einstein at the California Institute of Technology in January of 1933. Father Lemaître, priest and physicist, had challenged Einstein's postulate of a static state universe. Father Lemaître contended that an expanding universe, exploding from a "primeval atom" or "cosmic egg" actually sustained Einstein's general theory. Others were not convinced, and a decade later, in that dark mill of science which is Cambridge University, Arthur Eddington rejected it, and Fred Hoyle called Lemaître's theory the "Big Bang" as a term of mockery. But Einstein was deeply moved and said at the conclusion of Lemaître's presentation, "This is the most beautiful and satisfactory explanation of creation to which I have ever listened."

Beauty. Now, it was not Galileo, as many think, but Cardinal Baronius paraphrasing Augustine's insistence on the right use of reason who said that the Scriptures teach us how to go to heaven, not how the heavens go. But Augustine did confess, "Late have I loved thee, Beauty ever ancient, ever new." This was the ineffable beauty of the Creator, reflected in the symmetry of the entire universe. For all his

The Portsmouth Institute Conference, Portsmouth Abbey, Rhode Island, June 20, 2009.

theological constraints, it is significant that Einstein chose first to call Lemaître's explanation "beautiful".

This past March, YouTube delivered another powerful scene that, I admit, brought fugitive tears to my Anglo Saxon eyes. At Stanford University, an assistant professor of physics, Chao-Lin Kuo, knocks on the door of the Russian physicist Andrei Linde to tell him that many years of patient observation near the South Pole seem to confirm his theory of primordial gravitational waves issuing from the pure quantum gravity of Lemaître's "primeval atom". In astonishment, Linde's wife, also a physicist, speechlessly embraces the young man. Overwhelmed, Professor Linde accepts a glass of champagne and says hesitatingly, "I always live with the feeling—what if I believe this just because it is beautiful?"

If "beauty will save the world", pace Dostoyevsky, it will also salvage physicists, since beauty cannot contradict truth. And when physicists are allured, the heart of all science succumbs, for as Ernest Rutherford said, "All science is either physics or stamp collecting." Pope Urban VIII, who championed Galileo until that man, though of faith, made Simplicio in his *Dialogue of Two Chief World Systems* the weak proponent of divine omniscience, conjoined his patronage of science with that of art. For him, Galileo was not alien to those artists he also promoted: Bernini, Lorraine, Poussin, and Cortona. One need not fear hoping that a thing is true because it is beautiful. Truth cannot be ugly, and beauty is always a radiance of truth itself. Discord arises only when the categories are mixed up: when how to go to heaven is invoked to tell how the heavens go, or when knowing how the heavens go is applied to deny that we can go to heaven. Father Lemaître politely corrected Pope Pius XII for saying that his cosmological discoveries affirmed the "Fiat Lux!" of Genesis. The pope obliged the professor and backed off. On a lower level of discourse, the brilliant Father Stanley Jaki, who taught that modern physical science is the product of the Christian understanding of order and providence, corrected me once in a similar way, but not as delicately as Father Lemaître, for Father Jaki had a Hungarian spirit that did not tarry in the halls of patience or languish in understatement.

The list of great Catholic scientists is as long as the years since modern science became conscious of itself, but my clerical perspective would focus on Catholic priests compelled by beauty to discover more about the ordering of things, for, as Alexander Pope wrote, "Order is heaven's first law." Everyone knows of Roger Bacon and Albert the Great. But Copernicus was a priest, too, and likewise the geneticist Mendel. Barsanti developed the internal combustion engine after Buridan theorized inertial motion. Clavius was a guide in designing the Gregorian calendar; Gassendi observed the transit of a planet across the sun. Picard was the first to calculate accurately the size of the earth; Steno founded modern geology as Mabillon did paleography and Valentin modern chemistry and Mersenne acoustics. Sarasa increased our understanding of logarithms. Kircher was the first to observe microbes by microscope, and Jedlik invented the dynamo and electric motor. Thirty-five craters on our moon are named for Jesuits who contributed to natural science.

A particularly compelling model for the way the care of souls unites with the custody of creation is the singular prodigy Father Ferdinand Verbiest. He was born on October 9, 1623, the very day that Cardinal Maffeo Barberini, the future Urban VIII, wrote in a letter to Cesarini of the wonderful circumstance "in questa mirabil congiuntura" by which Galileo had supported Copernicus. Father Verbiest grew up in Pitthem, Spanish Netherlands, now Pittem, Belgium, and the homeland of Father Lemaître. Having studied in Bruges and Kortrijk, he studied philosophy and mathematics in Leuven, and then, having joined the Society of Jesus, he pursued theology in Seville and Rome, along with astronomy. His hope to be a missionary in Central America thwarted, he was sent to China along with thirty-five other missionaries and was one of ten survivors by the time the boat reached Macau in 1659. In the steps of Matteo Ricci and Adam Schall von Bell, the Jesuits had already established their presence in the imperial observatory in Beijing. Upon the death of their patron, the young Shunzhi Emperor, jealous court astronomers, led by Yang Guangxian, tortured them, and Verbiest was among those who were forced into a crouched position, unable to sit or stand for two months. Then sentenced to be cut to pieces while still alive, they were released after an earthquake and fire were taken as omens in their favor. Verbiest next submitted to several contests of his mathematical and astronomical skills, including the calculation of a lunar eclipse.

The new Kangxi Emperor made Father Verbiest his tutor in geometry, philosophy, and music. Father Verbiest was a priest first of all and secured permission to preach the Gospel throughout the empire, in return for translating the first six books of Euclid into Manchu. Some 800,000 conversions are attributed to his influence. Among his thirty published works is his translation of the Missal into Mandarin and *Kiao-li-siang-kiai*, a summary of the fundamental teachings of Christianity. He also reformed the Chinese calendar and calculated all solar and lunar eclipses for two thousand years. Ever the diplomat, but guiltless of human respect, when told not to correct the Chinese calendar he boldly answered: "It is not within my power to make the heavens agree with your calendar. The extra month must be taken out." And so it was. He rebuilt the imperial observatory and designed new instruments: an altazimuth, celestial globe, ecliptic armilla, equatorial armilla, quadrant altazimuth, and an eight-foot sextant. Using his surveying skills, and conferring in Latin with the Russian ambassador on behalf of the Qing emperor, he fixed the official Russo-Chinese borders. Rather like Aquinas dying after his magnificent brain was fatally wounded by a tree branch, Verbiest died in a fall from a bolting horse. He was given an imperial burial.

Verbiest had also studied the properties of steam. His "Astronomia Europea" describes an "auto-mobile" which he designed as a toy for the emperor around 1672. It used a rudimentary boiler (a prototype of the Stanley Steamer) with wheels turned by steam forced toward a turbine. This was a scale model not constructed to carry passengers, but while the invention of the car may be attributed to Cugnot, Anderson, Benz, or Daimler, and some have even proposed Leonardo earlier, there are those on the other side of their planet in remote Cathay who would say that the real inventor was Verbiest. More recently he was honored on a Belgian postage stamp.

Will Durant said, "Every science begins as philosophy and ends as art." These great priests in the name of Christ loved creation because of the Creator, and they never spent their intellects at the expense of the salvation of souls. They had no need to fear that their theories might be tricks because they were beautiful. Chimeras can fool the senses, but not beauty. And the Source of all beauty is Truth itself. "Out of Zion, the perfection of beauty, God shines forth" (Ps 50:2).

37

THE DRAFT RIOTS REVISITED

T HE STAIRCASE IN MY RECTORY is lined with pictures of the twelve pastors who preceded me in my parish, which is called Hell's Kitchen. I hope that thirteen is a benign number. While the neighborhood now is experiencing the most promising real estate development in the history of the nation, it did not get its nickname for being what it is now. Here is where the boatloads of Irish immigrants from the Great Famine arrived at the nearby docks, amid terrible poverty, crime, and vice, giving our vocabulary the "paddy wagon" and "donnybrook". The faces of my first predecessors are serious, for those pastors had a hard job to do for God, and I cannot hope to fill the shoes of those men who toiled in ill streets.

The first of them was Monsignor Arthur J. Donnelly, who built a huge parish from scratch in 1857, regularizing marriages and tending abandoned children and trying to form a Catholic culture just as Archbishop Cullen had managed to do somewhat in Dublin, where, contrary to romance, oppression had long neglected the moral norms of the Church. Donnelly was pastor during the Civil War and was appalled by what was happening to his people and nation as he tried to establish the parish. The great church, school, and convent that he established were moved a generation later two blocks north to make way for the Pennsylvania Station.

The Draft Riots took place July 13–16 in 1863. They had precedent in 1862, in Cincinnati where Archbishop John Purcell's brother, the Reverend Edward Purcell, was singular in his anti-slavery publicity through *The Catholic Telegraph*. Orestes Brownson, whom John Henry

Newman hoped might join his new Catholic University in Dublin, observed that pro-slavery Catholics for the most part "only acted out the opinions they had received from men of higher religious and social position than themselves" and insisted that, "if the general tone of the clergy and respectable Catholics of the city . . . had been decidedly opposed to the rebellion . . . , the riot never would have occurred, or . . . the chief actors in it would have been neither Irish nor Catholics."

In New York the riots lasted four days, and at least 120 were killed, while some estimates have five hundred or more. Over two thousand were injured, and more than fifty businesses and homes and two Protestant churches were destroyed. Racism melded with religious bigotry, and some Protestant churches were threatened because they were pro-Republican and centers of the abolition cause. Rioters sacked the Protestant "Five Points Mission" as a parish priest, at great danger to himself, tried to stop them while wearing his stole and waving his breviary. Two blocks from my rectory, a black man was lynched on a lamppost, mutilated, and set on fire. The nearby Presbyterian church was about to be torched when Monsignor Donnelly appealed to the mob, and the church was saved. Today at Mass I sit in a large oak chair that was the gift of the Presbyterian minister and his elders in gratitude for their rescue. When Monsignor Donnelly died in 1890 after thirty-three years as pastor, the Presbyterians attended his Requiem Mass, the first they had ever seen. Many of the overwhelmed police were Irish Catholics, horrified at what they saw, and they behaved heroically, like the local regimental Colonel Henry O'Brien, who was killed after trying to disperse the rioters.

However, as we have seen in recent times, race hustlers saw their opportunity to inflame the lower passions of men, and the mobs were encouraged by "community activists" from the Lower East Side and from as far as Philadelphia, with local gangs such as the Dead Rabbits, the Roach Guards, and the Forty Thieves, and the Plug Uglies and Blood Tubs from Baltimore. Some local Catholic pastors put themselves at risk, one stopping the looting of Columbia College, as did others in smaller riots in Hoboken, Hudson City, and Jersey City. Nothing stopped the burning of the Colored Orphan Asylum on Fifth Avenue between Forty-Third and Forty-Fourth Streets from which 233 children managed to escape just as the previous year dozens of black women and children barely escaped the torching of a tobacco factory in Brooklyn. The bishops of Buffalo and Cleveland issued pastoral letters, and one pastor in Troy saved a black church from arson. But these were unusual interventions. The great Fredrick Douglass, himself a former slave, who had spent six happy months in Ireland two decades earlier, inspired by the liberator Daniel O'Connell, lamented that "a people who so nobly loved and cherished the thought of liberty at home in Ireland could become, willingly, the oppressors of another race here."

The riots, which remain the worst civil insurrection in our nation's history, were barely mentioned in New York on their 150th anniversary. They were precipitated by the iniquitous Conscription Act the previous March, which allowed exemption from the newly imposed draft upon payment of $300, which was the annual wage for many laborers. Rich men like the fathers of Theodore Roosevelt and Franklin Delano Roosevelt paid the fee easily. Irish soldiers were over 15 percent of the Union enlistment, and the carnage was terrible. However, feelings also were fueled by resentment at emancipation and fear that black laborers, especially longshoremen, would take jobs from whites. Sentiment was exacerbated by Catholic journals, such as the *Freeman's Journal and Catholic Register* and the *Metropolitan Record*, in which, an editorial by Archbishop John Hughes had declared in May 1861 that slavery existed by the "Divine permission of God's providence".

The supposed chief hero of it all was in fact slow to address the scene. Archbishop John Hughes had come to America from County Tyrone and was employed as a gardener and stonemason in Maryland, where the Jesuits long before had owned a large slave population. The future bishop of New York, John Dubois, was then the head of Saint Mary's College in Emmitsburg and rejected his application for seminary studies. Elizabeth Ann Seton persuaded Dubois to take him in, since Hughes' lack of academic qualifications had not been his fault, given the Irish Penal Laws, but there was also a distinct difference in personalities. Dubois had been educated in the classical tradition in Paris under the Sulpicians, having also been a schoolmate of, remarkably, the revolutionaries Robespierre and Desmoulins, at the Collége Louis-le-Grand. During the French Revolution, Robespierre respected their old school tie and actually helped Dubois escape.

Dubois was the only non-Irish Ordinary in the history of New York, suffering much at the hands of those who considered his erudition the

stain of a "foreigner". They complained that he did not speak English well—this in spite of the fact that he had been tutored in English by Patrick Henry, and his eloquence impressed James Monroe,
to whom he had been introduced by Lafayette. It must not have been
easy for him to have been assigned Hughes as his coadjutor in 1838,
especially as Hughes, called "a tyrant, but with feeling", harbored a
habit of not forgetting a grudge. Later, Hughes berated the local laity
for their mistreatment of Dubois, but it could be said that his animus
was more against the trustee system that Dubois had also opposed.
The old Frenchman asked to be buried under the sidewalk so that the
people could "walk on me in my death as they did while I was alive".
Hughes obliged him with unseemly meticulousness.

One biographer said that Hughes was "impetuous and authoritarian,
a poor administrator and worse financial manager, indifferent to the
non-Irish members of his flock, and prone to invent reality when it
suited the purposes of his rhetoric". If he was a "fool for Christ's sake",
he generously supplied the raw material. He enjoyed the grand stage,
as when he threatened to turn New York into "a second Moscow" if
any church were attacked by the Know-Nothings. The grandiloquence
was rather vacuous since, although there were ignorant anti-Catholic
bigots like Samuel Morse and P. T. Barnum rumbling in New York,
the real torchings were in Philadelphia. In 1843–1844 Hughes toured
plantations in the South and Cuba, and on his return he preached in
Old Patrick's Cathedral on the virtues of the slave system. While slavery was "an evil", as he had written in a youthful poem, he decided
that it was "not an absolute and unmitigated evil".

Hughes went so far as to oppose the Free Soil movements and asked,
in defense of slave masters, "Is not the father of the family invested with
the power of God that he is sovereign, commanding and expecting to be
obeyed as he should?" The archbishop's sister, Margaret, had married
into the Rodrigue family, which had fled the 1793 slave rebellion in
Haiti. She helped instill in her brother a fear of the race she thought as
tempestuous as they were inferior. When the Civil War broke out, he
wrote to the pro-slavery Bishop Patrick Lynch of Charlestown, South
Carolina, a native of County Fermanagh, agreeing with him on states'
rights, and in May 1861 he declared that abolition violated the United
States Constitution and demanded that Lincoln should resign from the
presidency should he free the slaves. A great friend was William Se-

ward, and he regretted that Seward had lost the Republican nomination to Lincoln. Seward was "the only one in the cabinet of Mr. Lincoln fit to be at the helm". Seward kept a portrait of Hughes in his house, which he told some Nativists was Washington in his Masonic robes.

Through Seward's influence, in 1861, Hughes received a presidential commission to tour Europe in advocacy of the Union, which he patriotically defended, apart from the slavery issue. Privately he wrote to European merchants warning them that abolition would hurt their commerce. His trip is often cited as a valiant success, which to some degree it was with Napoleon III, although France was unlikely to turn against the Union. He received a federal expense account of about $118,000 in current exchange and then asked to extend his travels for another six months at a higher fee, which Lincoln rejected. Much is made of Lincoln's hint to the Holy See that Hughes be given a special honor, interpreted as the Red Hat. It is quite unlikely that Lincoln was fluent in such ecclesiastical matters, and Cardinal Antonelli may have sensed that Seward had proposed this at the prompting of Hughes, who was a man not without ambition. The request was ignored.

The Draft Riots were the darkest blot on the Church in the United States until the modern sex scandals and their concomitant episcopal dereliction of duty. Some polishing of reality has been attempted to vaunt Archbishop Hughes as a hero who saved the day. But Mayor Fernando Wood (himself a Confederate sympathizer) and other civic officials had been pleading with Hughes to do something, and he did not act. Finally, he responded to an appeal from Governor Horatio Seymour.

The archbishop's residence then was on the corner of Madison and Thirty-Sixth Street, which still exists, although the balcony has been removed and a beauty parlor and optical shop occupy the ground floor. On Thursday, July 16, unwell and wearing the toupee that had long been his gesture to vanity, which none of the faithful dared to remark, he appeared before four thousand, most of whom, he said, were not rioters, although some in the crowd sporadically shouted crude racial epithets, which the archbishop ignored. Amid the din, he chose to be humorous and elicited laughter with his jibes at the abolitionists and said virtually nothing about slavery but much by innuendo about his foes Horace Greeley of the *New York Tribune* and James Gordon Bennett of the *New York Herald*, never mentioning the attack on Greeley's office building. Previously he had condemned Bennett for being anti-Catholic, a wonderful charge since Bennett was a devout Catholic of the Scottish Highlands. But Bennett was a different sort of Celt. He did not please Hughes when once he remarked on the beauty of the Catholic solemn liturgies but unkindly added that to celebrate them properly among the "general run of New York Irish was like putting gold rings through a pig's nose". The crowd disbursed and the speech did not end the riots. The arrival in Murray Hill of the first of four thousand Federal troops, many bearing the scars of Gettysburg, did. Until then, through Thursday night, violence continued.

One case:

> Coroner Naumann held an inquest yesterday on the body of Wm. Henry Yates, a colored man, 41 years of age, who committed suicide at the house of his employer, James Martin, in Madison-street, by first cutting his throat, and then hanging himself to a cellar door by means of a small cord. The deceased resided in Water-street, and when the houses of the colored people were attacked by the mob on Thursday night, he undertook to defend his wife and children. The resistance which he offered was such as to excite them to the highest pitch, and many swore that he should be burned alive if caught. He secreted his family in the best way possible, and when resistance became hopeless he ran to the house of his employer where he was soon after found dead in the condition above stated. (*New York Times*, July 18, 1863)

Offended that Hughes claimed to have saved the day, Greeley charged Hughes with having helped foment the chaos and pointed out that if he had indeed been able to quell the riots, he should also have been able to prevent them. Greeley mocked Hughes for having supported conscription, but not "coercive conscription", and asked "Was there any other kind?" On Friday, Hughes wrote to Seward: "The plea of the discontents is, on the surface, the draft. At the bottom, however, in my opinion, the discontent will be found in what the misguided people imagine to be a disposition on the part of a few here and elsewhere to make black labor equal to white labor."

Lord Macaulay said, "There were gentlemen and there were seamen in the navy of Charles II. But the seamen were not gentlemen, and the gentlemen were not seamen." To make myth oblige fact, it may be said of the Draft Riots that there were heroes and prelates in the New York of 1863, but for the most part the heroes were not prelates and the prelates were not heroes. Or so it seems when one looks at the pictures of those old pastors in Hell's Kitchen.

38

MAD INTELLIGENCE

N INE YEARS AS CHAPLAIN of an eight-hundred-bed state mental hospital taught me that one can be mentally ill and highly intelligent. Talking with the patients often was more interesting than talking with their psychiatrists. Mad men are not mindless. They just do not distinguish between delusion and fact. Chesterton summed this up by aphorism: "The madman is not the man who has lost his reason. The madman is the man who has lost everything except his reason." This explains why it is often hard to distinguish university faculties from mental wards, save for the latter being kept under lock and key. Hitler, Stalin, Pol Pot, and their paladin in malice Chairman Mao were intelligent men who vandalized the attics of culture because they absorbed some vestige of that culture and thought it was rational to hate it.

Thus it is to a lesser degree with those who now advertise themselves as the cultural elite. That can be a noxious conceit, made worse by the perfume of popularity. At a recent conference, I was introduced as a "public thinker". It was meant as a compliment, but I demurred, replying that the term is vague and, from my own experience, the only "public thinkers" I know are those poor souls I frequently see on the New York City subway talking to themselves. Public thinkers such as politicians and members of the media who comment on them are the first generation of our society to have been badly schooled without being aware of the fact. I do not deny that many of them may be intelligent, but their mental acuity was disserved in the post-World War II generation by an ignorance of history. Napoleon had the same problem, which is why Talleyrand lamented that a man so highly intelligent had been so poorly educated.

Public thinkers have been usurped by practical atheists, who are politely styled "secularists". Essentially, the secularist is not without religion: rather, he has made a religion of politics and wealth and rejects any religion that worships anything else. Now, to be secular is unavoidable for anyone who resides on this planet, except for astronauts, and even they have to come back down to earth. But secularism distorts secularity, just as racism makes a cult of race. The secularist makes a religion of irreligion and is different from the saints, who are "in this world but not of it", because the secularist is of the world but not rationally in it. This explains why the secularist's solutions to the world's ills are so destructive. The secularist is isolated from what is unworldly and thus lacks the perspective that adequately measures things of this world. In contrast, Saint Paul was a most worldly wise man and not least of all because he knew of a "third heaven" where a man, possibly himself, "heard things that cannot be told, which man may not utter" (2 Cor 12:4).

The contemporary attacks on Christianity, moral and political, are redolent of the Decian persecutions, and yet an instinct of much of the secularist media is reluctance to report, let alone condemn beyond formulaic protocols, the beheading of Christian infants, the crucifixion of Christian teenagers, the practical genocide of Christian communities almost as old as Pentecost, and the destruction to date of 168 churches in the Middle East. Very simply, this rhetorical paralysis betrays a disdain for Judaeo-Christian civilization and its exaltation of man in the image of God with the moral demands that accrue to that. Their operative philosophy, characteristic of those who are empirically bright but morally dim, is that "the enemy of my enemy is my friend." There is, for instance, the alliance of the inimical Pharisees and Herodians to entrap Jesus (Mt 22:15–16). That is the logic of the asylum, where very smart people are also very mad. For Christ the Living Truth, it is worse than clinical insanity: it is, using his dread word, hypocrisy.

Many European sophisticates, such as the "Cliveden Set", cast an indulgent eye on the Nazis. Even some prominent Jewish voters and other minorities supported them, until the Nuremberg Racial Laws of 1935. This was so because the Nazis were seen as a foil to the Bolsheviks and a means to social reconstruction. Conversely, many Western democrats over cocktails supported the Stalinists because they were perceived as the antidote to the Nazis. The U.S. ambassador to the

Soviet Union, Joseph Davies, 1936–1938, wrote a book, *Mission to Moscow*, that whitewashed the blood on the walls of Stalin's purges. In 1943, with the active cooperation of President Roosevelt, Warner Brothers made it into a film that was hailed in the *New York Times* by Bosley Crowther for its unique "boldness" in coming out "sharply and frankly for an understanding of Russia's point of view." If the Nazis seemed an antidote to the Bolsheviks and vice versa, those unleashed bacilli nearly destroyed the world. Satan is a dangerous vaccine.

Secularists play down Islamist atrocities because they seek to eradicate the graceful moral structure that can turn brutes into saints. Heinous acts are sometimes dismissed as "workplace violence". There even are those in high places who pretend that Islamic militants are not Islamic and foster the delusion that false gods will not demand sacrifices on their altars. These elites are like Ambassador Davies, who said, "Communism holds no serious threat to the United States." Naïve religious leaders who live off the goodwill of good people will even say that Christians and those who oppose them share a common humane ethos, a similar concept of human rights, an embrace of pluralism, and a distinction between political and spiritual realms. Secularists who imagine good and evil as abstractions do not consider the possibility that hatred of the holy will take its toll in reality. By ignoring the carnage committed by the twentieth century's atheistic systems, they fit the definition of madness as the repetition of the same mistake in the expectation of a different result.

That mad kind of intelligence is offended by the precocious audacity of Winston Churchill writing in *The River War* at the age of twenty-five: "Individual Moslems may show splendid qualities. Thousands become the brave and loyal soldiers of the Queen: all know how to die: but the influence of the religion paralyses the social development of those who follow it. No stronger retrograde force exists in the world." For the secularist whose religious crusade against religion does not understand the world or its history, prophecy is the only heresy, and his single defense against false prophets is feigned detachment. Indifference is the fanaticism of the faint of heart. By not taking spiritual combat seriously, and by seeking an impossible compromise with the opposite of what is good, human wars cannot be avoided. There are different kinds of war, and only prudence tempers both pugnacity and pacifism. James Russell Lowell opposed the Mexican War and approved the Civil War, but with a sane intelligence: "Compromise makes a good umbrella, but a poor roof; . . . it is a temporary expedient, often wise in party politics, almost sure to be unwise in statesmanship."

If some unruly Presbyterians had flown airplanes into the World Trade Center and the Pentagon, secularist observers would have eagerly been searching Calvin's *Institutes* to find the roots of such misanthropy. Instead, in our present circumstance, confronting the abuse of truth and reason by the enemy of their enemy, secularists would rather sink into denial, like Ambassador Davies telling his wife, Marjorie Merriweather Post, that the gunshots outside were just the blasting for the new part of the subway. To deny the ultimate truth of Christ, who suffered for others in an inversion of the habit of carnal men to make others suffer, is to deny the economy of salvation itself. The Qur'an (Sura 4:157-58) says of Jesus: "They killed him not." Saint Paul says, "For many, of whom I have often told you and now tell you even with tears, walk as enemies of the cross of Christ" (Phil 3:18).

39

SERENITY IN STORMS

Who then is this, that even wind and sea obey him?

—Mark 4:41

I N GALILEE THERE WAS A STORM and the waves of the sea shook the fishermen's ship. What they called a sea was a lake, and what they called a ship was a boat, and what they called a storm was one of the countless storms that have rattled the world; but to die is to die, whether on a lake or a sea, whether in a boat or a ship, whether by one storm or all the tides and turnings of the universe. Through it all Jesus lay on a cushion asleep. The men woke him: "Teacher, do you not care if we perish?" Jesus rose. The men had awakened eyes that never sleep. Jesus did not rebuke the men. He rebuked the wind. How does one rebuke the wind? Did he groan or shout or cry a language unknown to us? He stared at the violent waves like a mechanic looking at a noisy machine: "Peace! Be still!" The sea became like glass. Everyone here knows what storms are and how many kinds there are. "Doesn't God care that we are dying?" Rebuke the winds, and they still blow. Only one voice can make "Peace" by saying "Peace".

Frightened as they were of the storm, the fishermen were more frightened when the storm stopped. "And they were filled with awe,

Prayer service for President George W. Bush, President George H. W. Bush, their families, and members of the government. Church of Our Saviour, New York City, September 2, 2004.

and said to one another, 'Who then is this, that even wind and sea obey him?" Who is this? He is more than we are.

Our beloved nation has been through many storms. Today different races and ways of believing gather here, but all of us stand on the same acres where, in this month of September in 1776, the American Revolution ended almost as soon as it began. The king's soldiers landed near where Thirty-Fourth Street is and captured eight hundred American soldiers. Soldiers? They were mostly farmers and shopkeepers. But they were soldiers because they would protect their country. George Washington galloped from Harlem Heights down to these streets. He rarely showed emotion, like the noblest of the ancient Romans. He had what some modern commentators with newly acquired Latin call *gravitas*. It means serenity in storms. General Washington seemed to lose it when he saw the New York militiamen panicking. In one of the few recorded instances of Washington shouting, he cried out, "Are these the men with whom I am to defend America?" He struck some of them with the broadside of his sword, but they fled. An officer grabbed his bridle and pulled him away from the enemy that within moments could have captured him and ended the American dream. Right here.

Washington was a great man, but he was only a man, and he could not rebuke the wind. His men fled. But they were good men, like the fishermen of Galilee. They came back. We are here today because they came back.

"Are these the men with whom I am to defend America?" Yes, General Washington. These are the men. They are all you have.

Three years ago our nation suffered a terrible storm. Some thought God slept. "Does he not care that we are dying?" Some of us saw many things on September 11. In one moment in the midst of a big crowd running from the smoke, a young couple were pushing a carriage. The baby was calmly asleep. Like Jesus in the boat. Priests looked into the eyes of firefighters asking for final absolution before they went into the flames. Those eyes keep looking at us, for they will never close. "Are these the men with whom I am to defend America?" Yes. These are the men, and these are the women, and these are the children of all creeds and races who cannot rebuke the winds themselves but who have a God who can.

When asked what kind of government we had been given, Benjamin

Franklin said, "A republic, if you can keep it." He meant virtue. There is no freedom without order and no order without virtue. Mockery of virtue has become an art form, and the anti-hero is called a hero. G. K. Chesterton saw this already in the early twentieth century, for he said: "The decay of society is praised by artists as the decay of a corpse is praised by worms." In classical Corinthian halls and great Gothic halls and bombed out halls of Parliament in the Battle of Britain, across the ages that divided them and in languages peculiar to each, Aristotle and Thomas Aquinas and Winston Churchill said this: "Courage is the first of virtues because it makes all others possible." Courage is the ability to react to the threat of harm rationally. Because it is rational, it requires caution, but caution, says Aquinas, is the prelude to an action, not a substitute for an action: if you want to be sure that your boat will never sink in a storm, you should never leave port. The cynic for whom all righteousness is only self-righteousness also calls courage bravado. True courage is the right use of reason in the face of evil.

Evil. We remember a man with a noble soul who was ridiculed for calling an evil empire evil. Ronald Reagan rebuked it, but he knew that only God had the power to rebuke it and bring it down. He said: "There are no easy answers, but there are simple answers. We must have the courage to do what we know is morally right." There is right and there is wrong, and in our weakness we may confuse right with wrong and wrong with right, but God is never wrong and always right, and so he can rebuke the winds. No mortal man or woman may call any other mortal man or woman evil, but everyone has a moral duty to call evil evil.

In the nineteenth century a young man confessed his sins to a peasant priest in the village of Ars in France, Saint John Vianney. The floor began to shake, knocking the fellow over. Vianney picked him up, brushed him off, and said cheerfully: "Do not be afraid, my son. It is only the devil." The young man was impressed, but he admitted that he would never go to Vianney for confession again. It is only the devil. It takes courage to say that in the face of terrorism. It is only the devil. That is the simple answer, but it is hard to say.

There on the far corner of this church is a picture of Saint Thomas More, the *Man for All Seasons*. He coined two words: Utopia and Anarchy. There can be no Utopia in the storms of this world, and yet if the winds that blow are not rebuked there will be anarchy. Pope

John Paul II declared Saint Thomas the patron saint of statesmen and politicians. Harry Truman said that a statesman is a politician who has been dead ten or fifteen years. That is not quite what the pope meant. He said that Thomas More teaches that "government is above all an exercise of virtue. Unwavering in this rigorous moral stance, this English statesman placed his own public activity at the service of the person, especially if that person was weak or poor; he dealt with social controversies with a superb sense of fairness; he was vigorously committed to favoring and defending the family; he supported the all-round education of the young."[1]

The first letter I ever received was sent to me by my father during the Second World War. He was sailing on a Liberty ship of the Merchant Marines on the Murmansk Run. His letter was addressed to me care of my mother because I was still in her womb. He told me to be good. He said his ship had gone through some storms and U-boats kept circling around, but "everything is fine." That was the clarion voice of a great generation, albeit censored in a time of curfews and measured silence. Some call it the greatest generation—so far. Mr. President, exactly fifty years ago today your father survived the crash of his aircraft and saluted the crew that rescued him. His generation was not so long ago, for he is here with us today.

In our day, stormy controversies attend questions of biotechnology on the micro level and world politics on the macro level. The answers are not easy, but they are simple: Everything will be fine so long as human rights respect the rights of God. The deepest question is, "Why did God make you?" The simplest answer that calms every storm is this: "God made me to know him, to love him, and to serve him in this world, and to be happy with him forever in heaven."

[1] John Paul II, Apostolic Letter issues Motu Proprio *Proclaiming Saint Thomas More Patron of Statesmen and Politicians*, October 31, 2000, no. 4.

40

BEHOLD YOUR MOTHER

AMONG THE THINGS HIDDEN from the learned and the clever are the glories of heaven. There are glories of human intelligence and design on this earth, but the eternal glories of heaven are revealed to children, who have no desire to outwit God. The child expects God to be God. God's heaven is no stranger than God's earth. To a child, gates of wood and gates of pearl are equally wonderful, and a sea of water and a sea of crystal are both remarkable only in that they are seas. Our Lord says, "Unless you turn and become like children, you will never enter the kingdom of heaven."

Our first ancestors did not have childhoods, being born fully formed from the dust of the ground and the side of man. So great was their intelligence that they could delight God by reason as happily as children can delight God by lack of reason. Yet intelligence is no vaccine against pride. Adam and Eve did not want to be like children, for the cleverness of evil had persuaded them to want to be like gods. They could not be like gods, but they did stop being like children. Those who will not be childlike will be childish. Adam hid behind a tree because he was ashamed of himself. To be childlike is to love God. To be childish is to envy God.

Our God could have come to us any way he wanted two thousand years ago. He willed to come down from heaven through a human mother because we can only go to heaven through a human mother. The heavenly Jerusalem is mother of us all who have received the

Funeral of Dorothy Elaine Albinson Rutler, January 31, 2001.

gift of life in the womb of a woman. Saint John, writing the Book of Revelation, saw "a great multitude which no man could number, from every nation, from all tribes and peoples and tongues . . . before the throne and before the Lamb, clothed in white robes, with palm branches in their hands" (Rev 7:9).

Our Lord offers the same gracious greatness to every generation by giving all of us the same mother. From the Cross in unspeakable pain, covered with blood, he said to you and me: "Behold, your mother."

Once my mother and I were looking at a famous painting of Mary weeping at the foot of the Cross. I went on about the artist, his style, his treatment of light, the composition, symmetry, and palette. When I finished, my mother said, "It must have been so hard for her." Mine was the eye of a critic; hers was the eye of a mother.

Thirty years have not dimmed my recollection of a night at the opera with my parents. We were close enough to see that the baby the soprano was holding was a doll, but when in a traumatic scene she dashed it to the ground, my mother let out a cry that could be heard by the prima donna. I was young enough then to be embarrassed. I am old enough now to know that such a cry has been the salvation of whole civilizations.

A while before my mother died, her mind began to grow tired. Often at the end of a day, she would seem to be imagining things that were not there. At sunset she would look at me and ask, "Where are the children?" She had been one of nine children and had cared for many. But she was not imagining what was not there. She could see that childhood itself is missing from the very life of our culture. This was a long memory, of Rachel weeping for her children who were not. Our Lord had some officious followers who wanted to prevent children from seeing their Messiah. He said, "Let the children come to me, do not hinder them; for to such belongs the kingdom of heaven."

Though very gentle, my mother would not tolerate anyone's criticism of four persons: the pope, because he is the pope; the queen, because she is the queen; the late Terence Cardinal Cooke of New York, because my parents were the last he received into the Church before he died in 1983; and Mother Teresa of Calcutta, because she was such a good mother.

I once listened to a conversation between Mother Teresa and my mother at a meeting in the Bronx. They were like two neighbors chatting over a backyard fence. It was so cheerful and spontaneous and natural that it seemed childlike. When my mother was unconscious a few hours before her death, I sang to her some of the hymns she had taught me as a child. Then I whispered in her ear, "Mother Teresa, pray for my mother." My mother opened her eyes and said, "Love." As the power of the Most High overshadowed the Blessed Virgin, the Holy Spirit said in whatever music the Holy Spirit utters, "Love", and then Love himself was conceived in her womb.

My mother died in the hospital last Sunday at twenty minutes after one in the morning. The grandfather clock in her empty house stopped at the same moment. A theologian might be too intelligent and clever to think about that. A child would take it for granted.

The epitaph of John Henry Newman reads: "Ex umbris et imaginibus in veritatem" (out of the shadows and imaginings into the truth). Not near the truth or around the truth but into the truth. Christ is the truth. When he rose victorious over death, he stood on the shore of the Sea of Galilee at the moment before dawn. He raised his hands with holes in them, calling out to the apostles in their boat, "Children, have you any fish?" These were grown men and strong men, but when they heard him call, "Children", it was like heaven.